ROUTLEDGE LIBRARY EDITIONS:
URBAN STUDIES

Volume 6

THE ELDERLY IN
POOR URBAN NEIGHBORHOODS

THE ELDERLY IN POOR URBAN NEIGHBORHOODS

VALERIE SLAUGHTER BROWN

Routledge
Taylor & Francis Group
LONDON AND NEW YORK

First published in 1997 by Garland Publishing, Inc.

This edition first published in 2018
by Routledge
2 Park Square, Milton Park, Abingdon, Oxon OX14 4RN

and by Routledge
711 Third Avenue, New York, NY 10017

Routledge is an imprint of the Taylor & Francis Group, an informa business

British Library Cataloguing in Publication Data
A catalogue record for this book is available from the British Library

ISBN: 978-1-138-89482-2 (Set)
ISBN: 978-1-315-09987-3 (Set) (ebk)
ISBN: 978-1-138-89523-2 (Volume 6) (hbk)
ISBN: 978-1-138-89527-0 (Volume 6) (pbk)
ISBN: 978-1-315-17954-4 (Volume 6) (ebk)

Publisher's Note
The publisher has gone to great lengths to ensure the quality of this reprint but points out that some imperfections in the original copies may be apparent.

Disclaimer
The publisher has made every effort to trace copyright holders and would welcome correspondence from those they have been unable to trace.

THE ELDERLY IN POOR URBAN NEIGHBORHOODS

VALERIE SLAUGHTER BROWN

GARLAND PUBLISHING, Inc.
NEW YORK & LONDON / 1997

Library of Congress Cataloging-in-Publication Data

Brown, Valerie Slaughter.
    The elderly in poor urban neighborhoods / Valerie Slaughter
Brown.
       p.   cm. — (Garland studies on the elderly in America)
    Includes bibliographical references and index.
    ISBN 0-8153-2540-1 (alk. paper)
    1. Poor aged—Ohio—Cleveland—Social conditions. 2. Poor
aged—Ohio—Cleveland—Economic conditions. 3. Inner cities—
Ohio—Cleveland. 4. Social problems—Ohio—Cleveland.
5. Cleveland (Ohio)—Social conditions. 6. Cleveland (Ohio)—
Economic conditions. I. Title. II. Series.
HQ1064.U6O33 1997
305.26'0977132—dc20   96-46552

To my mother, Sally Mae Calloway Slaughter, who nurtures me like a well-tended garden, and to my son, Bacari Kahron Brown.

Contents

List of Tables

List of Figures

Preface

Inner-city neighborhoods are the predominant places of residence of minority elders in America. Many of these neighborhoods are documented centers of urban blight and neglect. Nationally, a substantial percent of the residents live at or below the official poverty level. Intuitively one would think that these living conditions would negatively impact the well-being of its residents.

Considerable research has been done to identify neighborhood influences on children's affective states, motivation, and behavior. This population, along with the elderly, are this nation's largest dependent groups. In contrast, little research has been done to determine what impact living among poor neighbors has upon older Americans, specifically upon their psychological well-being and neighborhood satisfaction.

Scholars and the public tend to look at the poor and impoverished neighborhoods as fraught with liabilities. However, as a child growing up during the '60s and early '70s in such a neighborhood with many elderly residents on the East Side of Cleveland, I saw that we tended to look at our human condition and neighborhood in ways that highlighted the assets. Yet, we were still aware of our neighborhood's liabilities and how they shaped our daily lives. This way of perceiving our situation and the existence of an elderly support network fostered hope and stimulated motivation to rise above our immediate circumstances. The elderly seemed to be very happy and involved in the neighborhood. They were a treasured neighborhood resource for younger people. But that was several decades ago.

Having received a concurrent education in nursing and sociology at the undergraduate and graduate levels, I was eager to use my sociological imagination to examine quality-of-life issues relevant to inner-city residents. I set out upon this endeavor both as a nurse and sociologist. As a Child Health Nurse Clinical Specialist during the late '70s to late '80s, I practiced in several of Cleveland's inner-city hospitals and community-based clinics. I cared for high risk infants, i.e., premature and/or low birth weight newborns, born to teenage mothers living in urban neighborhoods with high levels of poverty. Oftentimes in the hospital emergency room I nursed people who were criminally victimized and injured in those same neighborhoods. My observations and other data then suggested that the neighborhood conditions and residents' quality of life had steeply declined since my tenure in such a neighborhood.

It was during the late '80s that my professional activities became more focused on sociological theory and empirical research. As a sociologist I wondered: Do older Americans in poor inner-city neighborhoods today experience high residential satisfaction and psychological well-being despite witnessing at least four contemporary research-documented impediments: 1) the migration of middle-class neighbors and jobs to the suburbs, 2) increased geographical spread of poverty, 3) increased concentration of poverty within a given neighborhood, and 4) increased prevalence of social problems in inner-city neighborhoods? I conducted this study to answer that question.

As a proponent of person-environment interaction theory, a review of the relevant literature led me to formulate the Urban Ecological Model of Aging. In chapter one I discuss sociological theories for their failure to *jointly* account for related micro and macro-level events. The conceptual model for this study links and attempts to explain the relationship between micro-level phenomena—personal and housing characteristics, residential satisfaction, and subjective well-being; and macro-level phenomena—neighborhood poverty level, and six salient negative social conditions. These conditions are juvenile delinquency, victimization of neighbors, welfare dependency, unemployment, households headed by females without paternal financial support for the children, and teen births. Additionally, the concentration of elders living in the neighborhood is included in the model as a macro-level characteristic.

The Urban Ecological Model of Aging was empirically tested with community-dwelling older people in Cleveland, Ohio. Subjects were predominantly participants in local neighborhood Senior Citizens Center programs. Among the programs were congregate meals, meals-on-wheels and social activities. A questionnaire was administered via telephone to 196 people whose primary language was English.

Chapter two develops the rationale for the Urban Ecological Model of Aging. Research questions and hypotheses are presented in chapter three. Chapter four discusses the research methodology. Chapter five analyzes the data testing the model's ability to predict the satisfaction and subjective well-being of older Americans in these neighborhoods. Chapter six discusses future theoretical and research directions for the study of elders residing in increasingly poor urban environments.

Scholars have expressed tremendous interest in the aging, poverty and quality of life issues addressed in my contextual analysis of inner-city elders. The theoretical development of the Urban Ecological Model of Aging and the research findings were presented as papers at the Gerontological Society of America annual meetings in 1992 and 1993. The model and research findings were also presented at the "Working Group on Developing Community Measures Quality of Life Assessment Meeting" in 1993, sponsored by Emory University School of Public Health and the Centers for Disease Control and Prevention. Most recently an article detailing the conceptual model's development was published in *The Gerontologist*, August 1995.

The study and its findings have important implications for public policy. Based on study findings, the well-being of older Americans is tied intergenerationally to the quality of life their neighbors experience. Public policy measures targeted to improve the quality of younger people's lives—such as, employment opportunities supportive of a decent standard of living, and affordable housing—should also enhance elders' sense of well-being. Hence, public policy measures that are aimed at younger persons have latent benefits for the elderly. Identification of these benefits is important to fully plan and evaluate the effectiveness of social programs.

Acknowledgments

This study required a concerted effort from many sources. I wish to thank my former dissertation committee members: Drs. Kyle Kercher, Eva Kahana, Marie Haug, and Claudia Coulton. These scholars' contributions to the literature in subjective well-being, person-environment interaction theory, elderly physical well-being, and poverty provided a basis for my conceptual model and study. Their knowledge and guidance enabled me to produce a theoretically and methodologically sound study.

Certainly this study could not have become a reality without the elders who participated, a special debt is owed to them. Several people were instrumental in linking me to prospective study participants: John Barky, Janice Dziegel, Stella Elder, Kathleen Slater, Delores Lynch, Abraham Sheppard, Christine Bellamy, Allison Wallace, Cynthia Plagata, Phyllis Smith, Theresa Cooper, Connie Chambers, Marian Warren, Annie Hicks, Mariam Gibson, Kim Delargy, Nilda Cunninghan, Carol Tag, and Selina Burrucker.

Work on this project was made more pleasurable because of my research assistant, Judie Barker. Several colleagues read an earlier draft of this book and made critical comments for which I am most grateful: Dr. William Julius Wilson, Dr. Eugene Uyeki, Dr. Curtis Gooden, Professor Donald Jelfo, Dr. Dorothy Salem, and Mr. Roger L. Williams. Technical support for this project was provided by Drs. Mark Saling, and Julian Chow. Clerical assistance was provided by Mr. Garnet Barker, Ms. Janice Ball, and Ms. Deborah Noureddine. Mr. Mark Jelfo provided the graphics expertise.

Family and friends provided diversional activities when I needed it most: Joyce Baker, LeVeeta Barker, and Deborrah and Leonard Dobrzeniecki. I am especially grateful to my mother, Mrs. Sally Mae Calloway Slaughter for giving me a love for learning and for our elderly neighbors. My son, Bacari, is an unending source of support to me.

I owe a special thanks to the National Institute on Aging for awarding me the Minority Dissertation Grant that made this study a reality. And thanks to Ms. Tami Holcomb, Department Assistant, Sociology, who kept the grant records and made sure all respondents and vendors were promptly paid.

The Elderly in Poor
Urban Neighborhoods

I

Introduction and Problem Statement

Little is understood about the effects on the elderly of living in urban poverty environments. Researchers have treated poor geographic areas as monolithic instead of as heterogeneous entities. Poverty areas vary at least in terms of the extent and duration of poverty, and perhaps will thus have different impacts on elderly behavior and subjective well-being (Coulton, Chow & Panday, 1990). The elderly poor have been studied extensively to ascertain the impact of personal poverty on the individual, a micro-level analytical approach. Studies seldom consider the possible influence of poverty-area contextual factors, and do not form a link between micro and macro-levels of theory and analysis (Alexander & Giesen, 1987). Clearly such a link is an important and under-explored area for research.

Furthermore, when elderly living environments have been examined, the focus has been primarily on institutional settings, i.e., nursing homes, the immediate personal living space, and planned housing projects (Carp, 1975a; Kahana, 1982; Lawton, 1980a, 1985). What is clearly lacking are studies that examine simultaneously the effects, on community-based elderly, of personal characteristics, and aggregate "people characteristics" of the suprapersonal environment (Lawton, 1990; Lawton, Moss & Moles, 1984; Lawton & Nahemow, 1979). The suprapersonal environment (Lawton, 1980a) is made up of the aggregated people characteristics of all individuals physically proximal to the subject of analysis. For example, average Social Security benefits for elderly recipients residing in the subject's neighborhood is a suprapersonal environment characteristic.

PURPOSE

The purpose of this study is to identify how urban poverty environments, associated negative social conditions, and characteristics of elder vulnerability affect elderly residential satisfaction and subjective well-being (SWB) (see Figure 1). The negative social conditions of the urban poverty environments include measures of neighborhood juvenile delinquency, victimization of neighbors, unemployment, female-headed households, welfare assistance and teen births. In addition to the additive effects of characteristics of elder vulnerability and the suprapersonal environment on residential satisfaction and subjective well-being, interaction (non-additive) effects will also be analyzed in this study (see Figure 2). The interaction component of the model is the potential buffering effect of specific personal characteristics of vulnerability on the relationship between perceptions of the suprapersonal environment and subjective well-being. More specifically, the study will examine whether the impact of neighborhood poverty type on SWB is greater for persons who are more vulnerable due to lower income, female gender, minority status, single marital status, impaired physical function/ADL, less perceived social support, or less received social support.

MAJOR CONTRIBUTION

A major contribution of this study to the gerontological literature is its linking of macro (environment) and micro (individual) levels of social scientific theory and analysis. A predictive model of subjective well-being among community-based elders is presented and tested. Multiple suprapersonal environment and personal characteristics are included in the model. The implications of this study are of potential importance, given that the overwhelming majority of elders reside in the community, and social planning requires input on how environmental factors influence elder's subjective well-being.

Of added significance is the study's use of commensurate perceived versus objective measures of suprapersonal environment characteristics. The elders are asked their perceptions of extent and duration of poverty in their suprapersonal environment, the neighborhood. Additionally, objective, census-based measures of extent and duration of poverty are also considered. It is widely argued in the person-environment fit literature that commensurate objective and perceived measures should be used when examining person-environment interaction.

In the next chapter, the literature review is presented. The review provides theoretical and empirical support for the selected conceptual model, and addresses conceptual issues relevant to this research. Five areas of literature are discussed: 1) micro-macro sociological theory links; 2) person-environment interaction , specifically, the ecological model of aging; 3) poverty neighborhoods; 4) residential satisfaction; and 5) subjective well-being.

II

Theoretical Framework and Review
of the Literature

Sound research to advance sociological understandings requires a conceptual model that is theory-driven and subjected to empirical testing (Jasso, 1988). To formulate such models, theoretical and analytical issues in the particular realm of inquiry need to be openly addressed.

Toward this aim, five areas of literature are reviewed as the basis for the current study's analysis concerning the suprapersonal environment, and individual characteristic's effects on residential satisfaction and subjective well-being of older Americans. The areas are: 1) micro-macro sociological theory links; 2) person-environment interaction: the ecological model of aging; 3) poverty neighborhoods; 4) residential satisfaction; and 5) subjective well-being.

The ensuing literature review draws upon these five realms to provide theoretical and empirical support for the formulation of hypothesized relationships between selected key variables (see Figures 1 and 2). That is, the literature review provides the foundation for developing a testable model to explain the subjective well-being of elders living in urban neighborhoods with varying degrees of poverty.

MICRO-MACRO SOCIOLOGICAL THEORY LINKS

An innovative aspect of this research relates to its use of a conceptual model that emphasizes micro-macro links to understand elderly subjective well-being. These links are between the well-being of elderly individuals and the larger suprapersonal environment of the urban neighborhood. A brief summary of the micro-macro debate is in order at this time to enable the reader to better appreciate the significance of this linkage.

Historically, sociology has been concerned with a micro-macro debate over how to conceptualize its subject matter (Alexander & Giesen, 1987). The question at the heart of the debate is: In the context of social relations, is the primary focus of sociology to be on the social system (i.e., the large, complex scale of social reality and action), or is primary emphasis on the individual actor (i.e., a part of the social system)? Inevitably, the leap must be made to connect the macro and micro-levels, respectively, in order to interpret and explain social reality that is a product of the two levels. Increasingly, sociologists are endeavoring to discover ways to link societal and individual phenomena by articulating the mode of transition from one level to the other (Blau, 1987; Brewster, 1994; Coleman, 1987; Gerstein, 1987; Miethe & McDowall, 1993). This link is vital because one goal of theory is to direct empirical analysis, and quite often a problem arises when trying to meet this objective. A large amount of sociological research focuses on the individual as the unit of analysis, while theory is macro-tuned to the operation of the social system. The macro theory is not translated into a clear understanding of the individual level of the system. This gap between theory and research may be an indication that theory does not make available to the researcher a useful link to the individual. It is imperative that theorists and researchers endeavor jointly to bridge the gap.

In an attempt to lessen this gap, the current study has included subjective, objective, micro, and macro level constructs together in an empirically testable theoretical framework. For example, subjective well-being (SWB) is an individual feeling state (i.e., a subjective, micro-level construct). Furthermore, the present investigation examines SWB in the context of the suprapersonal environment of the neighborhood: 1) negative social conditions as perceived by the study subjects (i.e., subjective, macro-level constructs); and 2) neighborhood poverty type (i.e., subjective and objective, macro-level constructs).

Having concretely acknowledged the micro-macro debate and demonstrated briefly how it is addressed in this study, we now turn to the second area of literature, person-environment interaction theory. This theory is presented to operationalize the actual links between the elderly (micro) and their environment (macro), and show the implications of this association for SWB.

PERSON-ENVIRONMENT INTERACTION: THE ECOLOGICAL MODEL OF AGING

The broad theoretical background for this study is provided by person-environment interaction theory. This theory involves the potential vulnerability of the person and characteristics of the environment (Harel, Ehlich & Hubbard, 1990; Lawton, Windley & Byerts, 1982; Windley, Byerts & Ernst, 1975). There are three primary theoretical models of person-environment interaction: 1) the complementary/ congruence model (Carp 1976, 1983); 2) the congruence model (Kahana, 1982); 3) and the ecological model of aging (Lawton & Nahemow, 1973). The shared basic assumption of these models is that human behavior and psychological well-being are reflective of the interaction between the individual and the environment. Of these three models, the ecological model of aging, with modifications, has been chosen to provide the theoretical framework for this study because the model explicitly focuses on the suprapersonal environment and its potential effects on the individual.

Furthermore, the ecological model is a reasonable starting point given that the majority of gerontological research has implicitly or explicitly used this model (e.g., Biegel & Farkas, 1990; Lawton, Brody and Turner-Massey, 1978; Myers, 1978; Wiseman, 1980), to investigate the residential satisfaction of community-based elderly, their desire to move, and their SWB. Findings from the current study will be compared to prior studies that also use the ecological model to study predictors of subjective well-being. Social policy development regarding elderly health and welfare, as well as city planning and design relevant to elderly housing, have relied heavily on findings of social scientists using the ecological model (Lawton, 1980a, 1980b, 1985).

Before discussing modifications to the model for our research purposes here, a description of the original model is beneficial to better highlight its limitations. The ecological model of aging (Lawton & Nahemow, 1973) characterizes the person or individual as possessing various degrees of competence in four spheres: 1) biological health (e.g., amount and severity of chronic medical conditions); 2) sensorimotor functioning (e.g., ability to perform activities of daily living); 3) cognitive skill (e.g., ability to solve problems); and 4) ego strength (e.g., amount of self-esteem). The environment exerts presses, i.e., demands on the actor, such as stairs in the dwelling of a person with arthritis, thereby constraining or shaping behavior (e.g., confining activities to one floor in the home). Individual adaptive behavior and subjective well-being are said to be balanced when the demands of the environment (press) do not exceed the level of individual ability to manage the demands (competence). Continuing with the above example, balance is achieved when the person with arthritis, experiencing impaired competence in the spheres of biological health and sensorimotor functioning, manages to perform all activities on one floor of the home, and minimize stair climbing and pain. According to the ecological model, the person in this example has responded successfully to the press the environment posed.

Germane to the model is the potential for greater vulnerability, or compromised competence, of the elderly compared to younger age groups, especially elders with impoverished resources and multiple problems or needs. Compromised competence and environmental press generate problems or needs, and thus become additional sources of stress for the individual (Kahana, Kahana & Kinney, 1990; Lawton, 1990; Varghese & Medinger, 1979). The person is vulnerable or compromised to the degree that external and internal resources are insufficient to alleviate the stress, or reduce it to an innocuous level, thereby promoting well-being.

We see evidence of this vulnerability in the area of elderly housing (Lawton, 1980; 1990; Varghese & Medinger, 1979). Elders who are retired, widowed, black, receive federal assistance, or have limited financial resources, may in fact live in poverty (Biegel & Farkas, 1990; Jackson, Kolody & Wood, 1982; Morris, Crull & Winter, 1976; Watson, 1983). Poor elders are more likely to live in the inner city and substandard housing, than in the suburbs and good quality housing. In addition, many of the social ills associated with poverty are concentrated in the inner-city neighborhoods, e.g., high rates of juvenile delinquency, crime, unemployment, female-headed households with absent, non-supportive fathers, welfare assistance, births to teenage mothers, and poor housing quality (Brewster, 1994; Crane, 1991; Coulton et al., 1990; Lynn, Jr. & McGeary , 1990; Massey, 1990; Miethe & McDowall, 1993; Rodgers, 1996). These social problems are added stressors for the vulnerable elderly (McAdoo, 1983; McNeely, 1983;   Varghese & Medinger, 1979).

Lacking resources to improve their housing and neighborhood with which they may be dissatisfied, the elderly may suffer a decline in psychological well-being. Some of these older people may want to move because they are dissatisfied. But they are unable to move because of diverse circumstances including undesirable housing alternatives (Biegel & Farkas, 1990; Morris et al., 1976). The frustration created by the unfulfilled desire to move can also negatively affect well-being (Biegel & Farkas, 1990; Carp, 1975a, 1975b; Lawton, Kleban & Carlson, 1973; Wiseman, 1980).

Despite the tremendous efforts of gerontologists, there is a knowledge deficit in the person-environment relations literature as it relates to the elderly and their housing. In support of person-environment theory, empirical evidence shows that interactions between environmental presses (e.g., old dilapidated housing) and personal competencies (e.g., impaired physical function) get translated into dissatisfaction with one's housing and neighborhood, and a desire to move. The degree of residential satisfaction subsequently affects well-being (Diener, 1984; Galster & Hesser, 1981; Golant, 1982; Jirovec, Jirovec & Bosse, 1985; Larson, 1978; Lawton, Kleban & Carlson, 1973).

Additionally, researchers have only recently begun to analyze the influence of aggregate people characteristics (most commonly, age homogeneity influence) on elderly SWB. These investigators highlight the need for studying additional aspects of the suprapersonal environment that may influence the elderly (Kahana, 1982; Lawton, 1980b; Lawton, Moss & Moles, 1984; Lawton & Nahemow, 1979; Rosow, 1967), which this study attempts to do.

In sum, the current study, broadly conceptualized, examines person-environment transactions. The primary focus, however, is on the suprapersonal environment, and how personal characteristics of vulnerability interact with it (see Figures 1 and 2). Both person and environment dimensions are considered in a predictive model of SWB. As such, the ecological model of aging is an appropriate starting point for conceptualizing variable relationships. But this model has several limitations and, hence, requires major elaboration and modification to adapt it to our purposes here. The discussion will now focus on these model limitations and subsequent modifications undertaken in the present investigation.

ECOLOGICAL MODEL LIMITATIONS

The ecological model of aging has limitations in six areas when applied to the case of understanding well-being among the urban, community-based elderly. First, is the model's focus on the physical characteristics of the environment at the expense and neglect of the suprapersonal environment. The latter receives only cursory attention. Items in the physical environment, such as noise level, litter, transportation etc., are more closely studied for their effect on residential satisfaction and SWB, than the effects of the aggregated people making up the suprapersonal environment of the individual.

Second, even when attention is directed to the suprapersonal environment, the model fails to identify specific elements or domains of the suprapersonal environment thought to influence residential satisfaction and SWB. For example, age-similar peer influence on residential satisfaction and SWB has been more extensively studied than other suprapersonal environment characteristics. Identification of additional elements of the suprapersonal environment and their operationalization would ease application of empirical analysis to the model.

Third, it is unclear how strong the association is between *objective* aspects of the suprapersonal environment and *perceptions* of that environment. A related question is, how do these two different aspects of the suprapersonal environment —objective and perceived— influence residential satisfaction and SWB?

Fourth, the individual (micro phenomenon) is linked to an uncertain geographic area for the aggregate environment (macro phenomenon). That is, the respondents' ideas about what constitutes their neighborhood are relied upon when measuring aspects of the suprapersonal environment and outcomes of residential satisfaction and SWB. Neighborhood geographical boundaries therefore, are highly variable across individuals, which is likely to reduce the accuracy of the empirical relationship between environment and outcomes that researchers report.

The fifth limitation of the ecological model of aging developed by Lawton and Nahemow (1973) is that it has been applied to limited settings, i.e., planned housing, nursing homes and the dwelling unit of the respondent. This approach yields samples that are not representative of the aging experience for the majority of the elderly in the United States, who in fact live in non-institutionalized settings and non-planned housing (Lawton, 1990). And finally, the model does not specify the effects personal characteristics of vulnerability, e.g., physical handicaps, may have on the relationship between perceptions of the suprapersonal environment and SWB.

THE URBAN ECOLOGICAL MODEL OF AGING

Lawton and Nahemow's (1973) ecological model of aging has been modified to redress each of the above-cited shortcomings, and appears here as the Urban Ecological Model of Aging (see Figures 1 and 2; also see Brown, 1995). The modifications are as follows. First, at the gross level the urban model includes parameters about both the physical *and* suprapersonal characteristics of the environment.

Second, the urban model includes a more differentiated specification of suprapersonal environmental domains (see Figure 1). Two domains of the suprapersonal environment thought to influence residential satisfaction and SWB are the objective (official) and perceived estimates of extent and duration of poverty in the neighborhood, varying from low to high levels and short to long duration (see Figure 1). Additionally, there are some common negative social conditions associated with poverty that taken together comprise another domain of the suprapersonal environment (SPE). These negative social conditions are perceived neighborhood rates of: 1) juvenile delinquency; 2) victimization of neighbors; 3) welfare assistance; 4) female-headed households with absent , non-supportive fathers; 5) unemployment; and 6) births to teenage mothers. Perceived neighborhood age homogeneity, (i.e., high concentration of elders in the neighborhood) may enhance elders' residential satisfaction and SWB (Lawton, Moss & Moles, 1984; Lawton & Nahemow, 1979). The absence of elderly majority in the neighborhood and greater age heterogeneity may promote intergenerational conflict. Such conflict may arise if there are conflicting values between the elderly and younger age groups living in the neighborhood. Accordingly, age homogeneity is included in the present model as another domain of the SPE.

As a third modification, the Urban Ecological Model of Aging strengthens the links among the SPE and residential satisfaction (see Figure 1) by standardizing the neighborhood component underlying residential satisfaction and the suprapersonal environment. The neighborhood is defined as the official U.S. census tract in which the community-based elder lives. The geographical boundaries of the neighborhood are fixed and serve as a common point of reference when gathering data about the suprapersonal environment and residential satisfaction.

The fourth modification made by the urban ecological model is its depiction of the objective neighborhood characteristics that inform individuals' perceptions of the neighborhood. In this study, objective neighborhood characteristics are official rates of poverty and its duration in specific urban neighborhoods. The perceptions of the neighborhood are the individual's estimations of the extent and duration of poverty in their neighborhood. Because the suprapersonal environment has been precisely defined by the census tract, this relationship between objective characteristics and individual perceptions is clarified, and commensurate measures of environmental phenomena achieved.

And last, the urban ecological model provides for the interaction of specific characteristics of elder vulnerability to influence the relationship between specific characteristics of the suprapersonal environment and SWB (see Figure 2). Although Lawton and Nahemow's (1973) model provided for the interaction effects of personal characteristics of vulnerability on the relationship between the individual and environment, they focused on the individual physical and behavioral competencies in association with physical characteristics of the environment. Specific characteristics of the suprapersonal environment and other potential sources of elder vulnerability (e.g., lack of social support) were not detailed in their model.

In sum, the modifications included in the Urban Ecological Model of Aging (UEMA) will facilitate empirical testing of person-environment theory in non-institutional settings, thereby extending its application to less controlled and more heterogeneous environments by other investigators.

At this point the literature review turns to an examination of the suprapersonal poverty environment which is the central macro-level context of this investigation. The next section details the conceptualization of poverty environments and their suprapersonal characteristics.

HETEROGENEITY OF POVERTY NEIGHBORHOODS

The heterogeneity of poverty environments is germane to this study because the well-being of elderly residents in the urban setting is under investigation. Central cities in the United States are becoming largely the residence of people across the age spectrum who are unable to move to the suburbs or exurbs (Cantor, 1979; Wacquant & Wilson, 1989/1991). This includes the vulnerable elderly. The urban centers are experiencing increased poverty rates and prolongation of the length of time its residents are counted among the poor. As more residents join the ranks of the poor, the configuration of poverty quickly spreads geographically (Massey & Eggers, 1990).

Studies of elderly well-being have not sufficiently incorporated contextual effects. They often ignore the suprapersonal environment all together (Atchley, 1990). Although a few studies examine neighborhood or social area contextual effects on elderly neighborhood and housing satisfaction, desire to move, and well-being, these studies do not acknowledge the contextual effects of poverty (Campbell, Converse, & Rodgers, 1976; Galster & Hesser, 1981; Jirovec, Jirovec & Bosse, 1985; Lawton, 1980b; Lawton, 1990; Lawton & Nahemow, 1979; Ward, LaGory & Sherman, 1985). If poverty effects are studied at all, usually the emphasis is on the significance of personal poverty and not neighborhood poverty (Lawton, Moss and Moles, 1984; Lawton, 1985). Additionally, even when existing studies account for heterogeneity of poverty neighborhoods and their differential effects on the residents' SWB, only objective measures of the negative social conditions are used (e.g., Wacquant & Wilson, 1989/1991).

Neighborhood poverty is important to the current investigation because the day-to-day lives and futures of the neighborhood residents are shaped in part by the forces of poverty (Lynn, Jr. & McGeary, 1990). This influence of poverty may be experienced by elders *consciously,* e.g., expressed dissatisfaction with the quality of housing available in the neighborhood for low income people; or *unconsciously,* e.g., elderly are unaware that the check cashing exchange stores that have largely replaced conventional banking institutions in poor neighborhoods, charge unusually high fees to cash government checks, thus decreasing the income of the elderly using the service ("Inner-City Pirates," 1991).

Poverty Typology

Some researchers have begun to examine the heterogeneity of poverty environments. Coulton and her associates (1990) have developed a typology for concentration and duration of poverty in neighborhoods specifically for census tracts. This typology is used in the present study to analyze the potential impact of heterogeneous poverty environments on elderly residential satisfaction and SWB (see Figure 3, paths 1, 2 and 7). The typology complements the Urban Ecological Model of Aging because it delineates the contextual parameters of urban poverty environments.

The scheme of poverty environments incorporates three types of high poverty areas contrasted to one type of low poverty area. By convention, researchers use 40% as the landmark for a high rate of poverty (Wacquant & Wilson, 1989/1991; Coulton et al, 1990). *Traditional high poverty areas* have 40% or more of their residents living below the poverty level without interruption since 1970. *New high poverty areas* have a poverty rate of 40% that occurred between 1971 and 1979. *Emerging high poverty areas* are characterized as having 40% or more of their residents existing below the poverty level between 1980 and 1990. *Low poverty areas* have less than 40% of its population below the poverty threshold.

Official Determination of Poverty

Poverty can be defined in absolute or relative terms (Eggebeen & Lichter, 1991; Tienda & Jensen, 1988). Absolute poverty exists when there are insufficient resources to provide the minimum standard of food and shelter, the basic requirements for life maintenance. On the other hand, relative poverty is the absence of adequate resources to provide a standard of living comparable to the prevailing average in society as a whole.

The federal government uses the absolute poverty definition to derive its official poverty line or index. This is based in part on number in the household, number of children under 18 years of age, income and age of head-of-household (less than 65 years of age or 65 and greater) (Eggebeen & Lichter, 1991; Palmer, Smeeding & Jencks, 1988; Tienda & Jensen, 1988). Each year the index is calculated to reflect changes in the Consumer Price Index—the increased cost of goods and services. However, changes in the average standard of living are not factored into the computation. For 1991, when the present study began, the poverty level for a family of four was an annual income less than $13,400.00.

The amount of money a family is calculated to spend on food is multiplied by three and this is the poverty threshold amount. Previous data gathered by the U.S. Department of Agriculture demonstrated that the poor spend one-third of their income for food (Palmer, Smeeding & Jencks, 1988). Hence, the remaining two-thirds would have to cover housing and other living costs. Incomes below this level may be supplemented monetarily by federal and state programs and with income-in-kind, e.g., food stamps and Medicaid.

To determine the number of poor people in a given year, every March the U.S. Bureau of the Census surveys households. The cash income and size of each household is compared with the poverty index to calculate the number of poor. Note that income-in-kind is not counted when determining poverty status. In 1963, 34 million (20%) Americans were poor. In 1993, 39.3 million, approximately 15% of the American population, were poor (Rodgers, Jr., 1996). Thus, with this example, between 1963 and 1993, there was a decrease in the poverty rate, but not a decline in the number of poor.

The aggregated people characteristics of these urban neighborhoods yield a suprapersonal environment. Let us examine more closely the nature of this environment to see its potential importance to residential satisfaction and SWB.

Poverty and the Suprapersonal Environment

In 1987, 60% of the poor resided in metropolitan areas, primarily in the central city, followed by rural and suburban areas (Schiller, 1989). Minorities, regardless of income, are more likely to be found in urban areas; poor blacks and Hispanics are most likely to reside in central cities (Conner, 1992). Poor whites are found largely in the central city and rural areas.

Although poverty is more likely for the young than the old, the poverty rates of aged adults still exceed that of non-aged adults (Conner, 1992; Smeeding, 1990). Black female-headed elderly households have an extremely high poverty rate. The oldest-old housed in the community have the highest poverty of all adult age groups, especially black and Hispanic females. Males, regardless of race, are less likely to be poor than their female counterparts (Conner, 1992).

Commensurate with the increased concentration, spread, and prolongation of poverty, is increased levels of social problems associated with poverty. Urban poverty environments are plagued with negative social conditions including high rates of juvenile delinquency, victimization, unemployment, female-headed households, welfare assistance, and births to teens (Brewster, 1994; Coulton, Chow & Sering, 1991; Crane, 1991; Lynn, Jr. & McGeary, 1990; Miethe & McDowall, 1993; Rodgers, Jr., 1996). In the current study, these negative social conditions are anticipated to adversely affect elderly residential satisfaction and subjective well-being, as shown in Figure 3, paths 4 and 10.

Structural changes in the U.S. economy, especially post-1973 economic deceleration, have spawned misfortune for inhabitants of our urban neighborhoods. As the shift has transpired from high-paying, low-skill and semi-skilled manufacturing jobs to a dichotomized work force of low-paid, low-skill service and retail workers on the one hand, and higher-paid, higher-skilled information and service workers on the other hand, unemployment has been on the increase for these residents (Jaynes & Williams, 1989/1991; Wacquant & Wilson, 1989/1991; Wilson, 1987; Zinn, 1989/1991). People lacking high technical skill and knowledge are relegated to jobs that provide an income equivalent to below the federal poverty line or in the range of the near-poor income, 125% of the poverty threshold. And they are the more fortunate ones, as more and more urban residents join the ranks of the unemployed. Over time, the disparity between black and white unemployment rate has held steadfast at a ratio of 2:1 (Rodgers, Jr., 1996).

Nearly one-third of blacks are members of poverty-stricken households (Rodgers, Jr., 1996). Fifty percent of black families with children are headed by one parent, more often than not the mother (Jaynes & Williams, 1989/1991). Of these one-parent families, 59% were living below the poverty threshold in 1987, in neighborhoods where many of their neighbors shared their plight. Not surprisingly, these families have correspondingly high levels of federal and state aid dependency. Such adverse conditions appear to affect psychological well-being. Mothers on aid were found to have depressed expectations of themselves and their children regarding education, career/job attainment, and living free of welfare assistance (Schiller, 1989; Wacquant & Wilson, 1989/1991).

The ravages of poverty are even more devastating for blacks in neighborhoods of high crime, drug abuse and low employment. The incidence of arrest, conviction and imprisonment for criminal offenses is much higher for blacks than whites. This reality is demonstrated in the prison population, where blacks outnumber by four times their proportion in the general population (Jaynes & Williams, 1989/1991).

The national pool of victims is also disproportionately black for certain offenses. Blacks are two times more likely than whites to be the victims of robbery, auto theft and aggravated assault; and six to seven times more likely to be a homicide victim. Black perpetrators of crime, likely to be poor and living in impoverished neighborhoods, usually target a black soon-to-be victim who is middle income or near poor. Minority elderly have a much higher rate of victimization than white elderly. Risk seems to be also positively linked with the concentration of black residents in an area (McNeely, 1983).

Age concentration in the younger age groups has also been linked to suprapersonal environments of poverty. Coulton and her colleagues (1991) found that traditional high poverty areas have a greater proportion of children and the lowest of elderly, compared to new high, emerging high and low poverty areas. This finding has implications for elderly SWB, and is discussed in the residential satisfaction and subjective well-being sections in this chapter.

Residential segregation in urban neighborhoods occurs along the strata of class and race (Massey, 1990; Massey & Denton, 1993; Massey & Eggers, 1990). Middle class residents relocate to areas of less poverty leaving behind their poorer neighbors (Wilson, 1987; Coulton et al., 1991). Blacks, regardless of socioeconomic status, find fewer housing opportunities in predominately white neighborhoods than Hispanics and Asians (Jaynes & Williams, 1989/1991).

To summarize, the suprapersonal environment of poverty neighborhoods is characterized by, but not limited to, high rates of the following negative social conditions: female-headed households, unemployment, welfare dependency, victimization of neighbors, juvenile delinquency, and births to teens. Additionally, impoverished neighborhoods are heterogeneous with respect to age group concentration.

As noted in the previous review, research examining elder subjective well-being has addressed the contextual effects of the SPE in only a very limited fashion. The present study redresses these limitations by using: 1) a typology to account for heterogeneity of poverty neighborhoods; 2) a standardized neighborhood concept; 3) perceived as well as objective data on poverty neighborhood type; and 4) a specified set of negative social conditions for which perceived estimates are obtained from the respondents regarding the severity of these conditions in their given neighborhood.

Now the literature review shifts focus to the relationship between elderly satisfaction with living space, and its implications for subjective well-being, the final outcome of interest.

RESIDENTIAL SATISFACTION

The environment as delineated in the social gerontology literature has micro and macro-levels. The micro-environment is the person's dwelling or living space. The macro-environment is composed of the area encompassing the micro-level, i.e., the neighborhood, community, city, state, etc. These environments influence residential satisfaction and consequent psychological well-being (see Figure 3, path 6). Elderly satisfaction with their living environment has been investigated as residential, environment, housing, and neighborhood satisfaction, depending on the study. Oftentimes residential satisfaction is conceptualized to include both neighborhood and housing satisfaction, as well as desire to move (i.e., measured as a single composite scale). Therefore, this literature review examines residential satisfaction as a composite of these three areas—neighborhood and housing satisfaction and desire to move.

Jirovec, Jirovec and Bosse (1985) found four significant neighborhood predictors and one housing predictor of residential satisfaction among healthy, geographically stable male elderly living in urban settings. The predictors, respectively, are beauty, safety, stimulation level, quietness, and housing ventilation. Together these variables accounted for 56.6% of residential satisfaction.

Lawton (1980b) analyzed 1976 Annual Housing Survey (AHS) data obtained from interviews with 14,420 elderly headed households. He found generally high neighborhood satisfaction among all respondents, particularly owner occupants. Neighborhood satisfaction was somewhat lower for blacks, central city metropolitan area residents, and renters. Significant determinants of neighborhood satisfaction were feelings of security from crime, houses in good repair, minimum street noise, and the absence of trash, litter and junk (see also Lawton & Hoover, 1979). Neighborhood crime was of great concern for central-city residents, single-person households, and renters. In all, 18 neighborhood attributes accounted for only 19% of the variance in neighborhood satisfaction.

Golant (1982) found that age, income and education were not related to neighborhood satisfaction. The more satisfied elderly were generally happy people, and had lengthy tenure in their present dwelling—away from which they ventured infrequently.

Studying many independent and intervening variables, Galster and Hesser (1981) accounted for 25% of the variance in neighborhood satisfaction. They discovered that young, married, female head-of-household and black subjects reported lower residential satisfaction than other subjects. Residents indicating inadequate common-interest relationships with neighbors experienced significantly less neighborhood satisfaction than their counterparts.

Morris, Crull and Winter (1976) found that education, income, occupation and number of months married had statistically significant relationships to neighborhood satisfaction. Renters wanting to be owners, and subjects desiring and expecting to move were associated with neighborhood dissatisfaction.

Lawton, Brody and Turner-Massey (1978) discovered that 47% of housing satisfaction variance is explained by enhancement of neighborhood quality, increase in cheerfulness or pleasantness of the housing unit, and a move to smaller living quarters.

Analysis of well-being among 2,431 elderly residing in federal housing by Lawton and Nahemow (1979) provided evidence that three of the five social area factors identified—single-owned dwelling, age concentration and high housing values—were predictive of housing satisfaction. Housing satisfaction was also greater for relatively new tenants, older tenants (in terms of age), blacks and public housing residents.

Lawton (1980b) found housing satisfaction was high among residents who were married, white, male head-of-household, of high SES, and living in newer dwellings, but low among blacks and renters. High housing quality ratings were obtained from white, married, homeowners with high education, residing in recently constructed low-rise multi-unit dwellings in metropolitan areas. Although blacks were somewhat less pleased than whites with their housing quality, the displeasure was not as great as anticipated based on the low objective assessments of the physical quality of their dwellings. The most deprived groups, i.e., blacks, renters, and single person households, were lowest in housing quality, housing satisfaction and neighborhood satisfaction.

In a study by Galster & Hesser (1981), subjects rated housing satisfaction high when they had indoor plumbing, heating, a modern kitchen, multiple bathrooms and were in a single family dwelling. But SES was not a significant predictor of residential satisfaction.

To summarize, consistent personal predictors of residential satisfaction are ownership of dwelling, security from crime, lengthy residency, not wanting to move, things in common with neighbors, and being white. Consistent environmental predictors of residential satisfaction are good housing quality/appearance, and modern conveniences, e.g., multiple bathrooms and updated kitchen. These variables will be considered in the testing of the Urban Ecological Model of Aging.

The last area of literature for review here is SWB, the final outcome of interest, and its' relationship to elderly residential satisfaction, characteristics of elder vulnerability and the suprapersonal environment.

SUBJECTIVE WELL-BEING

Life satisfaction, morale, happiness and positive affect are constructs that have been summarized and treated as subjective well-being or psychological well-being in the social gerontology field for the past forty or so years (Larson, 1978). Larson found several consistent and strong related factors of subjective well-being across studies he reviewed. These factors are, in order of decreasing strength, physical health, SES, level of social interaction, marital status, and certain areas of a person's living situation. Higher degrees of subjective well-being are witnessed by people who have better health, higher SES (income, education and occupation), higher levels of social interaction, a marital partner, easily accessible transportation, and improved or modern housing. Demographics of age, sex, and race inconsistently influence SWB (also see Markides & Mindel, 1987; Schaie, Orchowsky & Parham, 1982; Ward, 1983).

Desire to move, relocation and age-similar peers for neighbors have been identified as factors that impact on well-being. Lawton, Kleban and Carlson (1973) found that inner city residents wishful of moving expressed significantly lower morale than residents not wanting to move. Carp (1975a) found elders who relocated to a new public housing facility were happier than their peers who remained in unsatisfactory living environments. These statistically significant differences in morale were sustained over a long time—eight years. Lawton, Moss & Moles (1984) discovered that there were positive effects on SWB when the elderly perceived their neighborhood to be a homogeneous environment with respect to age similar peers.

More recently, Watson, Clark and Tellegen (1988) reviewed research that suggests positive affect and negative affect are two relatively independent (uncorrelated) dimensions that underlie emotion. These authors contend that positive affect (PA) connotes level of enthusiasm, alertness and activity. And that Negative affect (NA) connotes a panoply of aversive mood states and levels, e.g., anxiety, fear and anger. Because emotion is the core of SWB (Kercher, 1992; Watson et al., 1988), the current study will focus on PA and NA as the two major SWB outcomes (see Figure 3).

The affective states of SWB have been chosen as the outcomes of interest in this study. Conceding that SWB is multidimensional, other domains of SWB, e.g., appraisal of self (self-esteem), morale, or life satisfaction could have been selected as the dependent variable. As conceptualized in the literature, these alternative dimensions of SWB are themselves multidimensional and sometimes include residential satisfaction. In this study, residential satisfaction is identified as a separate and specific domain of satisfaction. Additionally, the literature does not provide concrete guidance as to which SWB outcome among community elderly will be most sensitive to the contextual effects of the suprapersonal environment. This is an understudied area in social gerontology.

In conclusion, both personal and environmental predictors of residential satisfaction and SWB are important and included in this study. A viable direction for the research on elderly residential satisfaction and subjective well-being is the joint application of the Urban Ecological Model of Aging, which highlights the suprapersonal environment, and the Coulton et al. (1990; 1991) typology of poverty environments. This strategy allows for the identification of contextual predictors of satisfaction and well-being among urban elders, many of whom are minorities. This is clearly an underdeveloped area of inquiry (Jackson et al., 1982; Schaie, et al., 1982).

Based on available literature, this study expects to find that the degree and duration of poverty in one's neighborhood affects one's residential satisfaction and subjective well-being. This is most likely to be true for those elderly with few social, economic, environmental or coping resources to change their situation (Kahana, Kahana & Kinney, 1990; McAdoo, 1983; McNeely, 1983; Varghese & Medinger, 1979; Watson, 1983).

SUMMARY OF CHAPTER

Chapter two presented the theoretical and empirical underpinnings of the Urban Ecological Model of Aging, the conceptual model that forms the basis for the present study. The model is a modification of the ecological model of aging, and incorporates a typology of poverty neighborhood types. Modifications were made based on a review of relevant literature: 1) micro-macro sociological theory; 2) person-environment interaction theory; 3) heterogeneity of poverty neighborhoods and their suprapersonal environments; 4) residential satisfaction; and 5) subjective well-being. The Urban Ecological Model of Aging will be used to evaluate the effect of poverty neighborhood suprapersonal environment, other perceived neighborhood negative characteristics, and characteristics of elder vulnerability on the residential satisfaction and SWB of the elderly.

Chapter three introduces the questions and hypotheses directing the investigation. To further clarify hypotheses, the suprapersonal environment is characterized in terms of specific negative social conditions and neighborhood poverty type. Distinctions are made between objective and perceived evaluations of the same suprapersonal environment.

III

Research Questions and Hypotheses

This study proposes to examine the effects of the suprapersonal environment on the residential satisfaction and subjective well-being of elders living in an urban environment. An Urban Ecological Model of Aging (see Figures 1 and 2), was developed from person environment interaction theory, macro-micro linkage theory, and previous research. The model is applied here to answer the research questions posed.

In this chapter a discussion is provided about the 1) global questions and hypotheses propelling the investigation, 2) the characterization of the suprapersonal environment, 2a) the distinction between objective and perceived characteristics of the suprapersonal environment, 2b) objective and perceived determination of neighborhood poverty type, and 2c) the selection of specific negative social conditions in the neighborhood to be studied. This discussion provides the foundation for the research questions asked, associated hypotheses, and a more detailed rationale for variable selection.

GLOBAL QUESTIONS AND HYPOTHESES

A fundamental question at the base of this study is: Does the suprapersonal environment affect the residential satisfaction and SWB of the urban elderly? The global hypothesis is that the suprapersonal environment (SPE) does affect these outcomes. This relationship is depicted in Figure 3, paths 1, 2, 3 and 4. The impact of the SPE includes both objective and perceived measures. The distinction between objective and perceived measures is discussed in the next section of this chapter. The perceptions of neighborhood poverty type (path 2) are expected to have greater impact on residential satisfaction and SWB than objective measures (path 1). Furthermore, it is hypothesized that the effects of objective and perceived SPE characteristics on positive and negative affect follow indirect paths, as well as the direct paths just discussed. These indirect paths are through residential satisfaction (path 6).

A second question addressed in this study is whether characteristics of elder vulnerability affect residential satisfaction and SWB? The general hypothesis is that characteristics of elder vulnerability influence residential satisfaction and SWB directly (see Figure 3, path 5). Furthermore, elder characteristics of vulnerability should have an indirect effect on PA and NA through the intervening variable, residential satisfaction (see Figure 3, path 6). A third fundamental question this study addresses is: Is the impact of the SPE on SWB conditioned by elder vulnerability characteristics? Characteristics of elder vulnerability are hypothesized to condition the effects of SPE on SWB. This interaction influence is depicted in Figure 4, paths 1 and 2.

These three fundamental questions and associated hypotheses are further elaborated upon to yield research questions and hypotheses with greater specificity.

SUPRAPERSONAL ENVIRONMENT CONSTRUCTS

Objective-Perceived Distinction

A more detailed discussion of the difference between objective and perceived measures is beneficial to understanding hypothesized relationships. One of the innovations of this study is the acquisition of comparable objective and perceived measures of the same suprapersonal environment entity for hypothesis testing. This method was dictated by the literature and the Urban Ecological Model of Aging.

The suprapersonal environment characteristics construct germane to this analysis is made up of three subcomponents, 1) poverty neighborhood type, 2) negative social conditions associated with impoverished environments, and 3) neighborhood age homogeneity. The reader will recall from chapters one and two that the suprapersonal environment is comprised of the characteristics of aggregated individuals in the subjects immediate living environment. An example is the percentage of welfare recipients in the neighborhood.

An objective measure of the suprapersonal environment is compared here to the individual subject's perception of the same environment. The objective measure is provided by official data gathering agencies. The perceived measure is the estimate the respondent provides based on personal experience.

Determination of Poverty Neighborhood Type

Poverty neighborhood type objective measures are provided by the U.S. Bureau of the Census. The census provides objective measures of the percentage of people below the poverty threshold down to the census tract level. These data are available back to 1970. Coulton et al. (1990; 1991) have categorized and identified poverty neighborhoods (i.e., census tracts) according to extent and duration of poverty (see chapter two, for typology). This was accomplished using census data.

In this study the neighborhood is defined by the geographical boundaries of the census tracts (CT). Respondents were first told the boundaries of their neighborhood and then asked to give their estimates of the percentage of poor in their neighborhood, and how long this degree of poverty had existed. Hence, objective and perceived commensurate measures of poverty neighborhood type were obtainable.

Neighborhood Negative Social Conditions

The second subcomponent of the suprapersonal environment selected here is negative social conditions. Elderly perceptions of negative social conditions in their neighborhood are hypothesized to be predictive of their residential satisfaction and SWB as depicted in Figure 3, path 3. The literature shows that objective measures of some of the selected negative conditions, i.e., welfare assistance and unemployment, do affect residential satisfaction (Wacquant & Wilson, 1989/1991). However, to obtain perceived measures of these neighborhood negative conditions, the conditions must be salient for the respondents.

In order to measure a negative neighborhood social characteristic, the elder must be able to conceptualize, observe, and see the importance of the condition in terms of a percentage estimate. Accordingly, the negative social conditions selected are juvenile delinquency, victimization, welfare assistance, female-headed households, births to teenagers, and unemployment (see Figure 3, path 3). The researcher reasoned that these conditions are easily apparent or within the scope of elderly awareness. Therefore, subjects should be able to give reasonable estimates of these items.

These conditions are not only likely to be salient to respondents, they are also among the most prominent social conditions cited in multiple studies about the milieu of urban poverty settings (Conner, 1992; Coulton et al., 1990). In other words, these social problems would seem particularly likely to have tremendous major implications for elderly residential satisfaction, SWB, government social policy, and allocation of national resources.

A third component of the suprapersonal environment selected for study is age homogeneity (i.e., whether the neighborhood is mostly elderly). It is reported in the literature that age heterogeneity is characteristic of urban poverty neighborhoods, and that elders in age homogeneous environments report greater residential satisfaction and SWB (see chapter two for more theoretical discussion). Age homogeneity is selected as a variable to replicate previous study findings.

To summarize thus far, the reader has been informed of the basic questions and hypotheses for this study, how the components of the suprapersonal environment (SPE) were selected, what suprapersonal variables will be used, and how distinctions are made between objective and perceived measures of the same SPE. The focus of the chapter now shifts to the more highly specified research questions and hypotheses, with rationale.

SPECIFIC QUESTIONS, HYPOTHESES AND RATIONALE

The research questions and hypotheses are divided into main and interaction effects. Each hypothesis is to be tested while controlling for the effects of all other variables in the model.

Main Effects (see Figure 3 for all paths mentioned):
   Question 1. Does objective neighborhood poverty type have an effect on residential satisfaction and SWB?
   Hypothesis 1. Objective neighborhood poverty type affects residential satisfaction and SWB (path 1). It will have a

negative effect on residential satisfaction and PA, and a positive effect on NA.

Rationale. Wacquant and Wilson (1989/1991) found that residents of objectively high (i.e., extreme) poverty census tracts report less neighborhood satisfaction than residents in low poverty tracts. Although these researchers did not examine the influence of residential satisfaction on SWB, several other studies have been previously cited that show residential satisfaction to be associated with SWB.

Question 2. Does perceived neighborhood poverty type have an effect on residential satisfaction and SWB, and is that effect stronger than that of objective neighborhood poverty type?

Hypothesis 2. Perceived neighborhood poverty type affects residential satisfaction and SWB (path 2).

Hypothesis 2a. Further, the perceived neighborhood poverty type will be a better predictor of residential satisfaction and SWB (path 2) than objective neighborhood poverty type (path 1). The greater the perceived extent and duration of poverty, the less the residential satisfaction and PA, and the more the NA.

Rationale. The hypothesis appears intuitively correct. As perceived neighborhood poverty increases, SWB may decrease over time because coping mechanisms used by residents to manage the stress of living in impoverished neighborhoods may lose their effectiveness (Kahana, Kahana & Kinney, 1990). The resources become depleted and compromised SWB occurs. This scenario seems very plausible concerning elderly residents in high poverty neighborhoods.

Along with these sustained high rates of poverty is the dramatic increase in social problems associated with poverty. It would be increasingly difficult to maintain residential satisfaction and SWB in the face of escalating environmental deterioration in one's proximity.

Question 3. Do the negative social conditions associated with impoverished neighborhoods, i.e., a) juvenile delinquency, b) victimization of neighbors, c) welfare assistance, d) unemployment, e) female-headed households, and f) teen births, affect elderly residential satisfaction and SWB?

Hypothesis 3. The greater the perceived level of these negative social conditions in the neighborhood, the less the residential satisfaction and PA, and the more NA (path 3). There are six paths implicit within path 3, one for each of the negative social conditions: a) juvenile delinquency, b) victimization of neighbors, c) welfare assistance, d) unemployment, e) female-headed households, and f) teen births. Henceforth, these subpaths will be identified as 3a, 3b, 3c, 3d, 3e, and 3f, respectively (not depicted in Figure 3).

Rationale. The literature review showed that these negative social conditions are associated with impoverished neighborhoods. In American society today, it is very difficult for the cognitively intact elderly not to be aware to some degree of the deteriorating social conditions in inner-city neighborhoods. The mass media, particularly commercial-television news programs, provide extensive, daily coverage of problems in the inner cities. What some urban elderly may do as a coping mechanism is to downplay the severity of the problem or its personal significance as a means of stress management, because they may not have a viable option to move (Kahana et al., 1990; Wiseman, 1980). This behavior reduces the impact of negative objective data on personal perceptions of environmental character salience, hence improving SWB and its mediator, residential satisfaction (Carp, 1979; 1975a; 1975b; Lawton, 1980b; Lawton, 1985). This strategy may be successful for some time. But as the social climate continues to deteriorate, as it does with persistent poverty, coping mechanisms may become strained. The strain is expected to be evident as residential dissatisfaction and compromised subjective well-being.

Victimization of neighbors is substituted for crime in this study to be sensitive to a point that Coulton et al. (1990) make: "Further, the count of crimes is linked to the census tract in which they occur rather than the tract in which the victim or perpetrator lives. Thus, these measures provide only a rough estimate of the actual relationship between poverty and crime" (p. 91). We will learn whether or not perceptions of victimization of neighbors is a negative social condition associated with high poverty neighborhoods. Inclusion of this variable in the analysis will add new knowledge to the literature.

> *Question 4.* Do elders in perceived age homogeneous neighborhoods have higher levels of residential satisfaction and SWB?

Hypothesis 4. Elders who perceive their neighborhood to be mostly elderly will have greater residential satisfaction and PA, and lower NA (path 4).

Rationale. Lawton and Nahemow (1979), using census data to define whether neighborhoods have a majority of elderly (i.e., are age homogeneous for elders), found elders in age homogeneous neighborhoods reported greater SWB than those in age heterogeneous neighborhoods. More recently, Lawton, Moss and Moles (1984) found in their analysis of data from two national surveys that older persons who perceived their neighborhoods to be mostly elderly reported higher SWB. Further, even though subjects' perceptions of age-peer concentration in the neighborhood were over estimation's of the actual figures, the findings linking age homogeneity and SWB were duplicated when actual census data were used instead of the subjects' estimations of neighborhood age composition. The current study seeks to replicate the findings of these investigators using elders' perceptions of neighborhood age homogeneity.

Question 5. Do the vulnerable elderly experience less residential satisfaction and SWB compared to their counterparts, the nonvulnerable elderly?

Hypothesis 5. The vulnerable elderly experience less residential satisfaction and PA, and more NA, compared to their nonvulnerable counterparts. There are 13 paths implicit within path 5, for each of the characteristics of elder vulnerability: a) age, b) race, c) sex, d) marital status, e) education, f) income, g) ADL, h) perceived social support, i) received social support, j) dwelling age, k) tenure (home ownership), l) number of bathrooms, and m) length of residency.

Rationale. While the list of potential vulnerabilities is probably infinite, the literature shows the characteristics of vulnerability germane to residential satisfaction and SWB to be those variables cited above (Biegel & Farkas, 1990; Conner, 1992; Coulton et al., 1990, 1991; Dunkel-Schetter & Bennet, 1990; Jackson et al., 1982; Kahana et al., 1990; Krause, 1987; Larson, 1978; Lawton, 1980, 1990; Morris et al, 1976; Stack, 1974; Wacquant and Wilson, 1989/1991; Watson, 1983).

Question 6. Is residential satisfaction predictive of SWB?

Hypothesis 6. Residential satisfaction is predictive of SWB (path 6). Elders who are satisfied with their residence will have greater PA and less NA than dissatisfied elderly.

Rationale. Numerous studies have demonstrated this link between residential satisfaction and SWB (Carp, 1975a; Larson, 1978; Lawton, Kleban & Carlson, 1973; Lawton, Moss & Moles, 1984; Lawton & Nahemow, 1979). The current study will attempt to replicate these findings.

Question 7. Is there a relationship between perceived neighborhood poverty type and objective neighborhood poverty type?

Hypothesis 7. Perceived neighborhood poverty type will display a positive relationship with objective neighborhood poverty type (path 7).

Rationale. The literature suggests that objective evaluations are correlated in a positive direction with those based on individual perceptions (Lawton, 1983).

Question 8. Is there a relationship between objective neighborhood poverty type and perceived neighborhood negative social conditions?

Hypothesis 8. Objective neighborhood poverty type will display a positive relationship with each of the six negative social conditions: a) juvenile delinquency, b) victimization of neighbors, c) welfare assistance, d) unemployment, e) female-headed households, and f) teen births. Henceforth, these subpaths will be identified as 8a, 8b, 8c, 8d, 8e, and 8f, respectively (not depicted in Figure 3).

Rationale. The researcher did not find any studies that have examined the link between objective neighborhood poverty type and residents' perceptions about these six negative social conditions. The current study addresses this knowledge gap, and thus *a priori* identifies these conditions as salient for the residents. The researcher anticipates that residents will have perceptions about the severity of these conditions in their neighborhoods. It is reasonable to expect that these perceptions will have some basis in fact. Previously discussed literature does in fact show that objectively determined high poverty neighborhoods do have higher levels of these negative social conditions compared to low poverty neighborhoods (Conner, 1992; Coulton et al.,

1990; Coulton et al., 1991; Wilson, 1987). That is to say, perceptions should be reflective, to some degree, of reality.

> *Question 9.* Is there a relationship between objective neighborhood poverty type and perceived neighborhood age homogeneity?
>
> *Hypothesis 9.* Objective neighborhood poverty type will display a negative relationship with perceived neighborhood age homogeneity.

Rationale. Objectively determined elderly age homogeneity is more characteristic of low poverty and non-central city neighborhoods. Here again, no studies have looked at the relationship between perceived neighborhood age homogeneity and objective neighborhood poverty type. But given the fact that elderly age homogeneity is less characteristic of high poverty neighborhoods, and that perceptions of neighborhood characteristics should have some basis in fact, neighborhood poverty type is predicted to be negatively associated with age homogeneity. That is to say, as the objective level of poverty in a neighborhood increases, the elders will more likely perceive the neighborhood as consisting of mostly non-elderly residents (reflecting the objective age composition of the neighborhood).

Interaction Effects:

> *Question 10.* Is the effect of the suprapersonal environment on SWB greater for the vulnerable elderly?
>
> *Hypothesis 10.* If elders perceive their neighborhoods to have high levels of poverty, they will experience less SWB (i.e., less PA and more NA). This will be the case especially for the vulnerable elderly, i.e., a) females; b) blacks; c) singles; d) physically impaired; e) low income; and f) elderly lacking perceived and received social support (depicted in Figure 4, paths 1 and 2).

Rationale. The Urban Ecological Model of Aging, the conceptual model for this study, allows for the hypothesized interactive effects of characteristics of elder vulnerability on the relationship between the suprapersonal environment and SWB. There is a great body of gerontological literature supportive of an interaction between person and environment, and that the nature of the interaction is conditioned by factors of vulnerability (Biegel & Farkas, 1990; Galster & Hesser, 1981; Golant, 1982; Lawton, 1980a, 1980b; Morris et al., 1976;

Wiseman, 1980). This hypothesis was first more generally formulated by Lawton and Simon (1968) as the "environmental docility hypothesis".

The environmental docility hypothesis asserts that the more competent person is less influenced by environmental factors than a person whose competence is compromised. This suggests, in keeping with the interaction hypothesis, that elderly who have multiple characteristics of vulnerability and thereby experience compromised competence, are in jeopardy. They are at increased risk of being more adversely affected by the perception of social problems reflected in the suprapersonal environment of the inner city.

Numerous studies have provided substantive support of docility hypotheses with different outcome variables, e.g., income (Dowd & Bengston, 1978; Jackson, Kolody & Wood, 1982; Jackson & Wood, 1976; Varghese & Medinger, 1979), self-reported health (Dowd & Bengston, 1978; Jackson, Kolody & Wood, 1982), life satisfaction as an indicator of well-being (Jackson, Kolody & Wood, 1982), and substandard housing (Jackson, Kolody & Wood, 1982; Varghese & Medinger, 1979).

The present study builds on these previous studies. In this study several characteristics of elder vulnerability—females; blacks; singles; physically impaired; low income; and elderly lacking perceived and received social support—are considered for their interaction effect on the relationship between the suprapersonal environment and SWB. It is noteworthy that the type of environment considered here is the suprapersonal environment, as opposed to the physical environment (i.e., natural and man-made materials in the environment, such as number of bathrooms, or other dwelling characteristics); the latter has been more extensively studied. Additionally, when the SPE has been studied, the focus has been on objective measures of the SPE and not individuals' perceptions of the SPE.

In conclusion, the proposed study has the potential to contribute significantly to the gerontological literature on person-environment interaction. It provides the first test of the docility hypothesis using the above-stated wide array of suprapersonal environment factors and urban community-dwelling elderly. It is the first study to examine the impact of perceptions and objective data concerning the suprapersonal environment.

This research also adds to the literature on linking micro-macro levels theoretically and empirically. The individual is linked simultaneously to both 1) a physical environment (i.e., a personal dwelling space), and 2) a suprapersonal environment (i.e., neighbors). Each environment is predicted to independently influence residential satisfaction and SWB, while controlling for the effects of the other environment. Furthermore, the individual is linked to a suprapersonal environment that has been standardized by designating its specific boundaries.

SUMMARY OF CHAPTER

In this chapter research questions and hypotheses with rationale were presented after a discussion of: 1) characterization of the suprapersonal environment; 2) the distinction between objective and perceived characteristics of the suprapersonal environment; 3) objective and perceived determination of poverty neighborhood type; and 4) the selection of six specific negative social conditions in the neighborhood to be studied. Hypotheses were presented based on main effects and interaction effects.

The next chapter focuses on the research methodology used to test the hypotheses. The research plan and its implementation are discussed in great detail.

IV

Research Methodology

In this chapter the research plan and its implementation are discussed. Topics covered are 1) sampling procedures, 2) the instrument used to collect the data, 3) measures and their psychometrics, and 4) statistical procedures for data analysis.

SAMPLE

One hundred and ninety-six (196) subjects were interviewed by telephone. Subjects were non-Hispanic, black and white, male and female, non-institutionalized elderly residents of the City of Cleveland proper. No suburbanites were included in the study. Subjects were 60 years of age or older at the time of telephone interview, and spoke English as their primary language. The mean time to complete the interview was 26 minutes (SD = 9). Blacks numbered 62% and whites 38%. There were 83% females and 17% males. The mean age was 73 years, S.D. 8. The majority of respondents were widowed (52%), followed by married 18%, divorced 17%, single never married 7%, and separated 6%.

A less than high school education was characteristic of 63%, of whom 29% had completed 8th grade or less. The majority of subjects were retired, 55%. Twenty percent were retired and disabled. Most of the respondents lived alone, 61%, and 26% lived with one other person. Of the subjects who lived with someone, 60% were head of household. Renters, 54%, outnumbered owners.

In terms of dwelling type, 35% were apartment dwellers, 33% lived in a two-family house, and 31% lived in a single house. The majority of the respondents, 72%, lived in dwellings of five rooms or less, and one bathroom was the norm, 83%.

Most subjects, 78%, lived in dwellings 30 years of age or more. The average length of residency was 22 years, S.D. 17. Private housing was dominant, with 84% residing there, as opposed to public housing units. And 21% of the respondents had their housing costs subsidized by the government.

For the year 1991, one income source was the case for 58% of the respondents. Social Security was the sole source of income for 46%. Social Security was a source of income for 90%. Two sources of income were the case for 37%. Some subjects, 36%, refused to give an actual income amount. Of those reporting actual income dollars, 64%, the mean income was $6,568, S.D. $3,950. Only 8% refused to give an income range. Eighty-four percent (84%) had an income in the less than $10,000 range. Subjects were selected for study based on their location within specified census tracts. Census tracts were identified using the 1990 Street Address/Census Tract Guide for Cuyahoga County (Northern Ohio Data & Information Service, 1991a).

Cleveland has 35 Statistical Planning Areas (SPA), each made up of multiple census tracts. Census tracts in SPAs of less than 5,000 residents in 1980 (Downtown and Industrial Valley), or predominately Hispanic (Old Brooklyn), were omitted from sampling because of insufficient population and the potential language barrier to responding to the English–language questionnaire and English–speaking interviewers. The remaining 32 SPAs were stratified in terms of East Side or West Side location. In Cleveland the East Side is predominately black and the West Side is mostly white. Next, each SPA was again stratified such that the four different types of poverty census tracts— low poverty, traditional high poverty, new high poverty, or emerging high poverty—(Coulton et al., 1990) were sub-grouped together. There were 76 low, 17 traditional high, 18 new high, and 38 emerging high poverty census tracts, for a total of 136 census tracts from which to sample. Fifteen of the 17 traditional high and all of the new high poverty census tracts are on the East Side of town. Emerging high poverty census tracts were distributed unequally, 25 on the East Side and 13 on the West Side in a ratio of 2:1. Low poverty census tracts were also unequally distributed, the East Side had 38 and the West Side had 28. There are more people living on the East Side of Cleveland than on the West Side. A list of the tracts according to East and West Side location and poverty type were numbered 001 through 136, consecutively. Then a table of random numbers was used to select five tracts of each: Traditional high (5 East Side); New high (5 East Side); Emerging high (3 East Side, 2 West Side); and Low (3 East Side, 2 West Side). A total of twenty tracts were randomly selected from which subjects were to be drawn. Twelve of the 32 SPAs were thus sampled.

Help was elicited from the Western Reserve Area Agency on Aging (WRAAA). The WRAAA is an organization that coordinates government and private funding to community agencies providing services to community-dwelling elders. Among the services provided are congregate meals that are affordable, nutritious lunches along with opportunities to socialize with peers, at neighborhood Senior Citizens Centers. Another nutrition service is meals-on-wheels, which provides affordable nutritious lunches to elders in their homes. These elders are unable to attend congregate meals at the neighborhood center. The inability may be due to health, family obligation or other reasons. These community agencies are also referred to as contract providers.

Once the 20 tracts were selected, the local contract provider servicing each tract was identified. A list of elderly who reside in the pre-selected census tracts of interest, use the center's services or are known to the center was obtained for sampling, using seven methods. One, prospective subject names were obtained by the investigator when visiting the centers during the congregate meal time to ask for volunteers from the selected census tracts. Two, center personnel compiled a list of seniors in the neighborhood. These seniors used the congregate meal service, the meals on wheels service, or were known to outreach workers but did not use center services. These prospective subjects were contacted by center staff via phone, or home visit to obtain permission for the investigator to contact them. Third, the investigator sent flyers (see Appendices B and C) about the study with the lunches to homebound seniors in the meals on wheels program, and to neighborhood senior centers to post prominently for seniors to read. Fourth, flyers were distributed to seniors at congregate lunch time by the staff on days the investigator did not visit to make them aware of the survey, its legitimacy, and to enlist their participation as appropriate. Fifth, flyers were also included in the centers' newsletters.

Sixth, subjects were also obtained from a neighborhood settlement house. These subjects were those associated with an intergenerational program at the settlement house, as well as seniors known to the staff, but not a part of any formal settlement program. Lastly, a snowball technique was used whereby subject volunteers were asked to recommend peers from the neighborhood who were unknown to the given center. These subject recruitment strategies were designed to yield a sample as representative as possible of elderly living in neighborhoods characterized by different levels of poverty.

Twelve subjects from each list, according to pre-selected census tract, were to be randomly selected by blindly picking a starting point and contacting every third client to be in the study, until the sample size of 12 per tract (total of 240) was accomplished. There were to be 60 subjects per each of the four poverty neighborhood types. Unfortunately, the seven methods for subject selection did not provide a sufficient listing of clients for some census tracts. This, coupled with disconnected phones, illness, hospitalization and refusal to participate, resulted in a sample where some census tracts had fewer than the planned 12 respondents.

Telephone interviews were conducted by the researcher and her research assistant. The research assistant required minimum training given her background as a practicing licensed clinical psychologist. Her training, conducted by the researcher, consisted of orientation to the study and reading assignments from pertinent literature. She also visited some of the Senior Citizens Centers with the researcher to obtain names of prospective subjects. Initially, telephone interviews were conducted by the researcher while the assistant observed. Next, the assistant performed some interviews with researcher supervision. And finally, the assistant and researcher performed interviews independently. This strategy enhanced uniformity in technique across interviewers. Throughout the data collection period, both researcher and assistant conducted interviews.

It is not possible to give a complete accounting of elders refusing to participate because agency personnel contacting prospective subjects did not pass on to the researcher information about refusals. Personnel gave the researcher a list of clients consenting to be contacted by the researcher. As stated previously, the researcher also gathered lists of elders willing to participate. Of the 274 elders who were contacted to participate in the study by the researcher or her research assistant, 196 (72%) agreed and 78 (28%) refused. Among the refusals there were 53 females, 23 males and two of unknown gender. Those refusing due to illness numbered 30 (38% of refusals), three of these had Alzheimer's disease, and seven were hearing and/or speech impaired to the extent that they were unable to respond to the questions over the phone. There was one refusal because the elder did not speak English. The refusals according to objective poverty neighborhood type were: 12 traditional high poverty, 17 new high poverty, 25 emerging high poverty and 24 low poverty. More detailed information on refusals is unavailable.

The end sampling result was 196 subjects from 24 census tracts representing 12 SPAs (see Table 1) according to neighborhood poverty type: traditional high poverty with five census tracts, 55 subjects; emerging high poverty with 9 census tracts, 50 subjects; new high poverty with 5 census tracts, 37 subjects; and low poverty with 5 census tracts, 54 subjects. Nine emerging high poverty census tracts had to be sampled to get sufficient potential subject names (see Table 1). When a sufficient number of names could not be obtained from which to sample, that census tract was removed from sampling and another tract was randomly selected to replace it. Fourteen census tracts had to be replaced in sampling.

A single WRAAA contract provider services many census tracts. This decreased the number of centers to be contacted for subjects. Sixteen WRAAA service provider agencies and one community settlement house were visited by the investigator, oftentimes twice, to obtain the name, address and phone number of prospective subjects. Volunteers residing outside of the selected census tracts were thanked for their willingness to participate and informed that unfortunately the census tracts/ neighborhoods studied did not include theirs, but that the investigator hoped to study more Cleveland neighborhoods in the future. The elders were eager to be selected and give their opinions about their particular neighborhood.

Subjects were assured that their identity and individual responses were confidential and no identifying information would be included in the study results. Verbal consent was then obtained to proceed with the telephone interview. Subjects were paid $10 for their participation through funding provided by The National Institute on Aging Minority Dissertation grant received by the researcher. A check was mailed to their home and their social security number was required for this purpose (see Appendix A).

Based on this design, study findings are generalizable to inner-city, non-Hispanic black and white urban elderly whose primary language is English. Although subjects were gathered from community centers providing social services for the elderly (60+ years of age), the only eligibility requirement for many center services is that the person be elderly, defined by the federal government in this instance as 60 and older. Clients who voluntarily seek services of Senior Citizen Centers may do so out of economic need. Conversely, some clients are perhaps drawn to the centers not by economic need, but by companionship or other needs. Some agencies have a client-find service. Outreach workers visit homes and churches in the community looking for prospective clients to acquaint with the center services. It was anticipated that clients obtained using client find may be less economically needy, thereby providing greater sample heterogeneity and a less biased sample. Furthermore, the sample includes subjects who were not known to the community agencies, but were recommended by elders in the study who did use community agency services.

INSTRUMENT

A 92-item questionnaire (see Appendix A) developed by the investigator was administered to survey subjects in their homes via telephone. The mean time to complete the interview was 26 minutes (SD = 9). The questionnaire included: 1) characteristics of elder vulnerability, including demographics, health-related measures, perceived and received social support, and dwelling characteristics; 2) individual perceptions of environmental/neighborhood characteristics, including poverty neighborhood type, and negative social conditions in the neighborhood; 3) subjective evaluation of neighborhood satisfaction, housing satisfaction and desire to move; and 4) subjective well-being indices. Objective suprapersonal environmental characteristics were obtained from Coulton et al. (1990, 1991), whose primary sources are the Bureau of the Census, 1990 Census, and 1991 poverty estimates.

PRETEST

The questionnaire was pretested for ease of administration, item clarity and determination of average time to complete. Two separate pretest determinations were conducted. The first pretest group consisted of ten retired and working adults in the Greater Cleveland area, i.e., the inner city and surrounding suburbs. Items were revised as appropriate, and the questionnaire then pretested a second time.

The second group of twenty pretest subjects were selected on the basis of their similarity to the targeted sample to be drawn. These pretest subjects were 60 years of age and older males and females, blacks and whites from throughout Greater Cleveland who utilize congregate meal services. Congregate meals are the lunches provided to community-dwelling elders by their local senior citizens' program at a minimum cost, and seniors are given an opportunity to socialize with their age peers. The second group of pretest subjects were paid $10.00 for their participation, as were the actual study subjects. Payment was made possible by a National Institute on Aging Minority Dissertation Grant. The questionnaire took the elderly pretest subjects 15 to 20 minutes in general to answer. The instrument was now ready for administration to study subjects.

VARIABLES AND THEIR MEASUREMENT

Subjective Well-Being

Consistent with prior research, subjective well-being is measured as two distinctive dimensions: positive and negative affect. Watson, Clark and Tellegen (1988) contend that positive affect (PA) connotes a level of enthusiasm, alertness and activity. Negative affect (NA) connotes a multitude of aversive mood states and levels, e.g., anxiety, fear and anger. The positive and negative affect dimensions are essentially orthogonal (Alexander & Robinson, 1991; Diener, 1984; Kane & Kane, 1981; Kercher, 1992; Lawton, 1978; Liang & Whitelaw, 1990). Because research indicates PA and NA are *distinct* dimensions with *distinct* external correlates (Watson, 1983; Watson et al., 1988) the present study analyzes each separately. Selected items from the Watson et al. (1988) brief measures of positive and negative affect schedule (PANAS) scales were used to assess positive and negative affect (PA and NA, respectively).

Each scale consists of 10 adjectives to be ranked on a five-point scale. Watson and associates report that the instrument has a general alpha reliability of .88 and .87, respectively, for positive and negative affect; with a PA-NA intercorrelation of -.17. Kercher's (1992) research with an elderly sample showed that a shorter 10-item PANAS can be used with slightly less but still good reliability (alpha = .75 and .81 for PA and NA, respectively).

The current study also used a shorter scale to keep the total questionnaire telephone administration time to within 20 minutes. Initially, a 12-item PANAS was used, comprised of six positive and six negative adjectives. Subjects were asked the PANAS items in reference to the past two-months' time frame to minimize contamination of affect with personality trait (Kercher, 1992).

To reduce the likelihood of respondents developing a set response to the PANAS items, response options were varied (see Table 6). Two groups of five options each were used to answer the PANAS items. For one group, the possible responses and corresponding scoring were 'not at all' (1), 'a little' (2), 'somewhat' (3), 'quite a bit' (4), and 'very much' (5). The possible responses and corresponding scoring for the second group were 'strongly disagree' (1), 'disagree' (2), 'neither agree nor disagree' (3), 'agree' (4), and 'strongly agree' (5).

Two additional items, one PA and one NA, were added to Kercher's 10-item short scale to achieve equal numbers of adjectives (3 each PA and NA) for each of the two groups of possible responses. PA and NA scores were tallied separately by adding the sum of the responses for PA items, and doing the same for NA items. Unstandardized scores were used, since the item variances within each scale were comparable. High scores on the PA and NA indicated higher levels of positive affect and negative affect, respectively. One adjective, "strong", was deleted from the PA scale because of its low correlation with the other PA items. The final modified version of the PANAS consisted of five PA and six NA items. A general alpha reliability of .72 was obtained for PA (see Table 6). The general alpha reliability for NA was .75, with a PA-NA intercorrelation of .28, $p < .001$. These findings and their implications will be discussed further in the last chapter.

Residential Satisfaction

The intervening variable is residential satisfaction. Residential satisfaction is multidimensional and includes 1) neighborhood satisfaction, 2) housing satisfaction, and 3) desire to move (see Table 6). The literature demonstrates that environmental influence gets translated into SWB through the path of residential satisfaction (see chapters 2 and 3 for more theoretical discussion).

To obtain information about residential satisfaction and other neighborhood characteristics, respondents were first told the geographical boundaries of their census tract (i.e., streets bordering the north, south, east and west) (Northern Ohio Data & Information Services, 1991b). In this study, the neighborhood was defined by the census tract. Subjects were then asked questions relevant to residential satisfaction.

The use of census tract geographical boundaries served to standardize the neighborhood concept and associated suprapersonal environment parameters for study subjects. This facilitated comparisons in the analysis of data. Lack of standardization of the neighborhood concept has been a major weakness in studies about residential satisfaction (Lawton, 1980a).

Neighborhood satisfaction was measured with three items, two of which were specifically about neighborhood satisfaction: 1) "To what extent do you feel your present neighborhood is a good place for you (and your family) to live?"; and 2) "I am dissatisfied with my neighborhood as a place to live". The third item concerned the quality of houses in the neighborhood: 3)"I rate the quality of the houses in my neighborhood as generally good." Housing satisfaction was evaluated with two items about level of satisfaction with the dwelling: 1) "How satisfied are you with your present house or apartment as a place to live?"; and 2) "I am dissatisfied with my house or apartment." Desire to move was measured using two items: 1) "How much do you agree or disagree with this statement: 'At the present time, I have no desire to move from where I'm currently living'"; and 2) "How much do you want to move at this time?"

Two five-point response categories ranging from 'strongly agree' to 'strongly disagree' and 'not at all' to 'very much' were used to measure subject response. High scores were indicative of a weak desire to move and great satisfaction with housing and neighborhood. Scales of this nature are frequently used in the literature (Galster & Hesser, 1981; Golant, 1982; Jirovec, Jirovec & Bosse, 1985; Lawton, 1980b).

An index of residential satisfaction was obtained by adding standardized scores of the items about housing and neighborhood satisfaction and desire to move. Standardized scores were used to give equal weight to each of the items comprising the index of residential satisfaction. Prior research provides support for this method for determining overall residential satisfaction (Jirovec et al., 1985). The residential satisfaction scale had a general alpha coefficient = .77 (see Table 6).

Poverty Neighborhood Type

Both objective and perceived (subjective) characteristics of poverty neighborhood type were measured (see Tables 5 and 6). As discussed earlier, Coulton and her associates (1990) have developed a typology for concentration and duration of poverty in neighborhoods, specifically for census tracts. At the onset of the study, Coulton et al. (1990) provide the objective neighborhood poverty type determination for each census tract in the study. Perceived neighborhood poverty type is measured by asking two questions: "What percentage of the people in your neighborhood do you think are poor?" and "Have these people become poor within (1) the past 10 years; (2) the past 11 to 20 years; (3) the past 21 years or longer?" Subject estimations of less than 40% poverty were scored low poverty, and estimations of 40% and greater were scored high poverty. Based on the response to the first of these two questions, all low poverty determinations were then classified as low poverty neighborhood type (consistent with the Coulton et al. typology).

High poverty determinations were further delineated as: 1) emerging high poverty neighborhood type, if the high rate was estimated to have been achieved within the past 10 years; 2) new high poverty neighborhood type, if the high rate was estimated to have been achieved within the past 11 to 20 years; and 3) traditional high poverty neighborhood type, if the high rate was estimated to have been achieved within the past 21 years or longer. The coding of the results from these two questions was: Low neighborhood poverty type = 0; emerging high neighborhood poverty type = 1; new high neighborhood poverty type = 2; and traditional high neighborhood poverty type = 3 (see Table 6; consistent with the Coulton et al. typology).

Negative Neighborhood Social Conditions

Six variables measured negative social conditions: juvenile delinquency; victimization of neighbors; unemployment; female-headed households; welfare assistance; and births to teens. Respondents, having been given the boundaries for their neighborhood, were asked "What percentage of the: a) youths do you think have been charged with juvenile delinquency; b) people do you think have been a victim of a serious crime (assault, larceny-theft, auto theft, robbery, murder, burglary, arson, rape); c) adults do you think are not working but are actively looking for work; d) adults do you think receive welfare assistance (food stamps, Medicaid/Supplemental Security Income, General Assistance, Aid to Families with Dependent Children); and e) female teenagers do you think had a baby last year"? (see Table 6).

Perceived Age Homogeneity

Perceived age homogeneity refers to the concentration of elders in the neighborhood. Subjects were asked which age group was the largest in their neighborhood. The options were: 1) children -- infant to 12 years old; 2) teenagers 13 to 19; 3) middle adults 41 to 64; and 4) older adults 65 and older. Perceptions of the neighborhood as mostly 65 and older was reflective of age homogeneity, with respect to the elderly (see Table 6).

Demographic Variables

These variables were coded as follows (see Table 6): Age (date of birth); sex (female = 1; male = 0); race (black = 1; white = 0); marital status (single, including those separated =1; not single = 0); education ("What level of education have you completed? (1) less than 4th grade; (2) 5th to 8th; (3) 9th to 11th; (4) high school; (5) some college; (6) BA; (7) MA or more); and income ("If not the actual dollar amount [asked of those refusing to give actual amount], then tell me in which of the following categories would you fall? (0) < \$2,500; (1) 2,501 - 5,000; (2) 5,001 - 10,000; (3) 10,001 - 15,000; (4) 15,001 - 25,000; (5) 25,001 or more)."

Physical Function/ADL

The measure of physical functioning was comprised of a six-item scale developed by Siu, Reuben & Hays (1990) on ambulatory geriatric patients. The scale is a combination of three established physical function scales: 1) the Katz Activities of Daily Living (ADL) Scale, 2) the Spector-Katz five-item Older American Resources and Services (OARS) instrument, and 3) the Rosow-Breslau Scale. Activities of daily living are arranged in this scale hierarchically from least to most difficult: dressing; bathing; getting to places out of walking distance; going shopping for groceries or clothes; doing heavy work around the house; and doing strenuous physical activities like hiking, tennis bicycling, jogging and swimming. This modified scale correlates highly with the established measures of subjective physical health, 0.63 - 0.89, $p < .05$ (Siu et al., 1990). The scale takes into consideration a wider range of physical difficulties ambulatory elders, such as some of those in this study, might experience. Subjects were to tell how much difficulty they had performing the six activities using a five-point scale ranging from 'none' to 'very much.' A high score on the scale means great physical function impairment. Based on this sample of urban elderly, the ADL scale had a general alpha coefficient of .87 (see Table 6).

Perceived and Received Social Support

It was anticipated that elders with greater social support would have greater well-being. Carol Stack (1974), in her seminal piece, described the importance of social support among the urban poor. Other researchers have more recently described the link of social support to residential satisfaction and SWB (Wacquant & Wilson, 1989/1991; Carp, 1975a).

Two dimensions of social support are included in this analysis. Perceived support is the aid people believe would be available to them if they needed it. Received support is aid that has actually been obtained (Dunkel-Schetter & Bennett, 1990; Cohen, Mermelstein, Kamarck & Hoberman, 1985). Based on an extensive literature review Dunkel-Schetter and associate (1990) show that there is a valid distinction to be made between perceived and received support, that these supports tap two distinctly different underlying constructs that share some moderate overlap.

Two scales of social support were created, using measures from established scales. The perceived social support scale consists of six items (see Table 6). One assesses overall perceived support availability and was the sole perceived support item used by Wethington and Kessler (1986). They found this single interval level measure to have "a significant modifying influence on the relationship between recent stressful events and psychological distress" (p. 80).

The remaining five items are from Cohen et al. (1985) Interpersonal Support Evaluation List (ISEL), the general population form. The ISEL consists of 40 items that comprise four subscales of the types of perceived social support: 1) "tangible"—perceived material aid; 2) "appraisal"—perceived availability of a confidant to discuss things with; 3) "self-esteem"—"the perceived availability of a positive comparison when comparing one's self with others" (p. 74 — 75); and 4) "belonging"—perceived availability of people to engage in activities with. The authors devised the scale to match the types of perceived availability of social support with specific coping requirements evoked by stressors. Theory supports the idea that perceived social support is viable and exerts a buffering effect when it meets the coping needs of the individual faced with a specific stressor.

For the sake of brevity, using telephone interviewing, the present study used five of the 40 items from the ISEL to measure perceived social support. The items from the subscales were selected as follows: tangible (2); appraisal (1); self-esteem (1), and belonging (1). These five items were chosen for several reasons. They tapped each of the four subscales. They captured the essence of multiple items that were not selected from the subscales. They were reflective of the type of aid that might actually be available in urban poverty environments. And they were indicative of the types of support people might see themselves needing to cope with specific problems. For instance, "If I were sick, there would be almost no one I could find to help me with my daily chores," is an included item. And an excluded item was "If I needed a ride to the airport very early in the morning, I would have a hard time finding anyone to take me."

For this sample of urban elderly the brief perceived support scale constructed had a general alpha coefficient = .68. The internal reliability of the entire general population ISEL ranges from .88 to .90, based on the two samples used by Cohen and colleagues (1985).

Another social support scale was created to measure received social support (see Table 6). Seven items were selected from Krause's (1987) modified version of the Inventory of Socially Supportive Behaviors (ISSB), which measures self-reported occurrences of helping activities. Krause contends that his scale measures perceived social support. But it actually assesses received support as defined by Dunkel-Schetter & Bennett (1990), Cohen et al. (1985), and Wethington & Kessler (1986). The items ask the frequency with which someone has provided social support in four domains: 1) Information support—knowledge given by others to aid the person to remedy a stressful situation; 2) Tangible support—physical items to be used to manage a stressful situation; 3) Emotional support—having a support person; and 4) Integration —being a source of support to others. Due to telephone interview time constraints, seven items were extracted from the 41 social support item list.

Three tangible, two emotional and two integration items were selected for use in this investigation. These seven items were chosen because they captured the essence of multiple items that were not selected from the subscales, and they were reflective of the type of aid elders in urban setting might have access to and have utilized. Three of the four subscales were sampled. Items were not selected from the informational support subscale because it was felt that informational support was implicit in the emotional support items selected. For example, an included emotional support item was "How often has someone been right there with you (physically) in a stressful situation?" The researcher felt that if this type of support had been received, it was likely to have been accompanied by informational support, such as, "Told you what they did in a stressful situation that was similar to one you were experiencing", or "Told you who you should see for assistance with a problem that you were having." These are informational support items on the Krause scale.

Two 5-item response categories were used: 'strongly agree' to 'strongly disagree' and 'never' to 'very often.' Items were stated negatively and positively. A high score indicated much perceived social support. An integration subscale item was deleted from the brief measure because it correlated poorly with the remaining received support items. The final modified scale used consisted of six items. Based on this sample of urban elderly, the brief scale of received social support has a general alpha coefficient of .69 (see Table 6). The reliability coefficients for these four subscales ranged from 0.67 to 0.83, as reported by Krause (1987). A total scale reliability coefficient was not reported.

Dwelling Characteristics
Several characteristics of a respondent's dwelling were measured: Length of residency ("How long have you lived in your present home?"); tenure ("Is your home rented or some other arrangement, or owned by you?"); dwelling age ("How old would you say your house or apartment is?"); and number of bathrooms ("How many bathrooms do you have in your house or apartment [including half bathrooms]?") (see Table 6).

Sample Descriptive Variables
There are additional variables that are not in the model, but were selected for sample description purposes and later analyses. These variables were not included in the model because they were not thought to be unequivocal predictors of well-being or residential satisfaction based on literature review. The variables are: 1) income source; 2) head of household status; 3) living alone or with other(s); 4) dwelling type – apartment, part of two–family, single home or other; 5) dwelling size—number of rooms furnished; 6) housing type—private or public; 7) non–subsidized or government subsidized housing.

DATA ANALYSIS

Ordinary least squares (OLS) regression analysis was used to test the Urban Ecological Model of Aging. Several tests were conducted beforehand to assure that assumptions of OLS regression were not violated. These tests were performed as specified by Norusis/SPSS (1990; pp. B-79 - B-88). No violations were noted.

Missing data in the regression analyses were handled with mean substitution. The negative social conditions had moderate numbers of missing data, and means substitution was used to maximize cases for the regression with the understanding that attenuated correlations might be the result. Using means substitution seemed reasonable given that subjects did not refuse to give estimates of the negative social conditions, they simply did not have an estimate to give. That is, the absence of an estimate implied the social condition was not salient to them and, therefore, was unlikely to affect their SWB. Hence, the attenuation of correlations resulting from substitution of mean scores for those subjects would be appropriate.

SUMMARY OF CHAPTER

In this chapter the research plan and its implementation were discussed. Specifically covered were 1) sampling procedures, 2) the instrument used to collect the data, 3) measures and their psychometrics, and 4) statistical procedures for data analysis. In the next chapter study findings based on the implemented research plan are presented.

V

Results

In this chapter the results of hypotheses' testing are presented. Presented first are the effects of the suprapersonal environment characteristics on residential satisfaction, Positive Affect (PA), and Negative Affect (NA). Presented second are the effects of the characteristics of elder vulnerability on residential satisfaction, PA, and NA. Next, the relationships between objective neighborhood poverty type and each of the perceived neighborhood characteristics are examined. Then, results are presented regarding the interaction effects of suprapersonal environment and elder vulnerability characteristics on PA and NA. There is also a separate section that focuses on the indirect effects of the predictor variables on the outcomes of interest. Lastly, serendipitous findings are noted at the close of the chapter.

SUPRAPERSONAL ENVIRONMENT CHARACTERISTICS

Hypotheses 1 and 2 both propose a link between neighborhood poverty type (objective and perceived, respectively), and 1) residential satisfaction, 2) PA, and 3) NA. The results in Table 3 indicate only very limited support for those hypotheses. Neither objective nor perceived poverty type has a direct effect on residential satisfaction, PA or NA. Additionally, of the two poverty types, objective neighborhood poverty type exerts indirect effects on residential satisfaction (-.07), PA (.09), and NA (.06) (see Table 4). These results also lead us to reject hypothesis 2a, which proposes that the effect for perceived neighborhood poverty type on residential satisfaction, PA, and NA, would be greater than the effect for objective neighborhood poverty type.

The results in Table 3 also indicate very limited support for hypothesis 3. The hypothesis suggests that each of the six negative social conditions (i.e., juvenile delinquency, victimization of neighbors, welfare, unemployment, female-headed households, and teen births) would have negative effects on residential satisfaction and PA, and positive effects on NA.

However, among the 18 possible direct effects derived from the six perceived neighborhood negative social conditions and the three outcome variables (residential satisfaction, PA, and NA), only three effects were statistically significant ($p < .05$). Perceived victimization of neighbors has a negative direct effect on residential satisfaction (beta = -.26). Perceived female-headed households has a direct positive effect on PA (beta = .23), opposite of the hypothesized direction. That is, the elderly residing in neighborhoods that have high purported rates of female-headed households exhibit significantly more PA. And perceived neighborhood unemployment is the only perceived negative social condition to directly influence negative affect (beta = .15).

Finally, perceived neighborhood age homogeneity (i.e., where elderly are perceived as the majority), is an SPE characteristic that hypothesis 4 suggests has a direct positive effect on residential satisfaction and PA, and direct negative effect on NA. The hypothesis is not supported because age homogeneity has no statistically significant ($p > .05$) effect on either residential satisfaction, PA or NA (see Table 3).

CHARACTERISTICS OF ELDER VULNERABILITY

Hypothesis 5 proposes a direct link between specific demographic, physical function/ADL, social support, and personal dwelling characteristics of elder vulnerability, and 1) residential satisfaction, 2) PA, and 3) NA. It states that the vulnerable elderly experience less residential satisfaction and SWB compared to their nonvulnerable counterparts. The results in Table 3 indicate stronger support for this hypothesis, than for hypotheses regarding suprapersonal environment (SPE) effects.

Statistically significant ($p < .05$) direct effects on PA were exerted by sex (beta = .15), income (beta = .19), and perceived social support (beta = .19). With regard to NA, statistically significant direct effects are exerted by sex (beta = .17), race (beta = -.32), ADL (beta = .19), and number of bathrooms (beta = .15). The direct positive effect that number of bathrooms has on NA is opposite of the hypothesized direction. That is, the elderly residing in homes with more bathrooms exhibit significantly more NA. Also statistically significant are the direct effects for perceived social support (beta = .19), received social support (beta = .23), dwelling age (beta = -.21), and tenure (beta = .21) on residential satisfaction.

In sum, four of the 13 characteristics of elder vulnerability influence residential satisfaction, PA and NA. However, with the exception of sex and perceived support, none of the predictor variables shows a relationship with more than one outcome variable. In other words, the three outcome variables have very different predictors as measured by characteristics of elder vulnerability — a result consistent with the findings for the effects of the SPE reported earlier.

RESIDENTIAL SATISFACTION

Hypothesis 6 suggests that residential satisfaction will have a direct effect on PA and NA. The results in Table 3 indicate a statistically significant (p < .05) effect for residential satisfaction on NA (beta = -.27), but not PA (beta = -.10). Hence, the results once again indicate that the predictors of PA and NA are distinct.

RELATIONSHIP BETWEEN OBJECTIVE NEIGHBORHOOD POVERTY TYPE AND PERCEIVED NEIGHBORHOOD CHARACTERISTICS

The zero-order correlations in Table 2 are supportive of the three hypotheses linking objective neighborhood poverty type with 1) perceived neighborhood poverty type, 2) perceived neighborhood negative social conditions, and 3) perceived neighborhood age homogeneity (see Table 2). All correlations are statistically significant (p < .05). Specifically, consistent with hypotheses 7, 8 and 9, respectively, objective neighborhood poverty type is predictive of a) perceived neighborhood poverty type (r = .37), b) each of the six negative social conditions (juvenile delinquency r = .31; victimization of neighbors r = .27; welfare r = .21; unemployment r = .28; female-headed households r = .37; and teen births r = .39), and c) perceived neighborhood age homogeneity (r = -.18).

INTERACTION EFFECTS

Hypothesis 10 proposes that the perceived neighborhood poverty type and selected elder vulnerability characteristics interact in their effect on SWB. The results in Table 3 show no statistically significant (p > .05) interaction effects for any of the seven product terms analyzed. Therefore, the results are not supportive of hypothesis 10.

INDIRECT EFFECTS

The results previously discussed concern the direct effects of predictor variables on residential satisfaction, PA, and NA. Table 4 presents total effects (including indirect as well as direct effects) for these variables. Although the hypotheses focused on the direct effects of predictor variables, some of these variables also exhibited statistically significant (p < .05) indirect effects, thus contributing to the variables' total effects.

Among the SPE characteristics, only objective neighborhood poverty type exerts an indirect effect on PA (beta = .09), through perceived neighborhood female-headed households. None of the elder vulnerability variables has indirect effects on PA.

Two SPE variables have indirect effects on NA. Perceived neighborhood victimization has an indirect effect via residential satisfaction (beta = .07). Additionally, objective neighborhood poverty type has an indirect effect on NA via perceived neighborhood unemployment and perceived neighborhood victimization (beta = .06).

Several elder vulnerability variables exert indirect effects on NA through the intervening variable residential satisfaction. The variables and their corresponding betas are: perceived social support (beta = -.05); received social support (beta = -.06); dwelling age (beta = .06); and tenure (beta = -.06). The only indirect effect on residential satisfaction is the influence of objective neighborhood poverty type via perceived neighborhood victimization (beta = -.07).

In sum, the additional information conveyed by the indirect effects confirms our earlier conclusion based on the direct effects. The suprapersonal environment variables have very few direct or indirect effects on PA, NA or residential satisfaction. Conversely, the elder vulnerability variables have a larger number of direct or indirect effects on the outcome variables.

SERENDIPITOUS FINDINGS

The results in Table 2 show PA and NA to be positively correlated, r = .28, for this sample of urban elders in impoverished and higher income neighborhoods. This is in stark contrast to reported studies of elders and younger age groups where there is no significant PA/NA association, or the association is negative (Kercher, 1992; Watson et al., 1988). Furthermore, the positive PA-NA relationship in the current study persists even when examined within various subcategories: income less than or equal to $10,000 (r = .32, n = 151) vs income greater than $10,000 (r = .16, n = 29); education 11th grade or less (r = .40, n = 123) vs high school grad (r = .18, n = 53) vs some college or more (r = .12, n = 19); male (r = .45, n = 33) vs females (r = .34, n = 121); low poverty neighborhood (r = .34, n = 54) vs emerging high poverty neighborhood (r = .25, n = 50) vs new high poverty neighborhood (r = .32, n = 37) vs traditional high poverty neighborhood (r = .22, n = 55); age less than or equal to 72 (r = .22, n = 109) vs age greater than 72 (r = .36, n = 87); and race black (r = .34, n = 121) vs white (r = .20, n = 74).

SUMMARY OF FINDINGS

Figures 5 and 6 provide an overview of the results for the direct and indirect effects of the suprapersonal environment and elder vulnerability characteristics on residential satisfaction, PA, and NA outcomes. As indicated in these two path diagrams, these three outcomes generally do not share the same predictors. However, for all three outcomes, the primary predictors stem from characteristics of elder vulnerability rather than the suprapersonal environment.

For residential satisfaction, the predictors comprising elder vulnerability are: perceived social support; received social support; dwelling age; and tenure. Furthermore, only one of the six negative social conditions from the suprapersonal environment, perceived neighborhood victimization, is predictive of residential satisfaction.

Likewise, the characteristics of elder vulnerability that predict PA are: sex; income; education; and perceived social support. And for NA, the elder vulnerability predictors are: sex; race; ADL; and number of bathrooms. In contrast, only one suprapersonal environment characteristic, perceived neighborhood female-headed households, is predictive of PA. And only one suprapersonal environment characteristic, perceived neighborhood unemployment, is predictive of NA.

Additionally, residential satisfaction is predictive of NA but not PA. Lastly, the suprapersonal environment and selected characteristics of elder vulnerability do not interact in their effect on PA and NA.

These findings based on the data analyses are discussed in the next chapter along with plausible alternative explanations for results contrary to study hypotheses. Suggestions for future research are also presented.

VI

Discussion

Several issues regarding the interpretation of results are discussed in this chapter. First, the suprapersonal environment influences on residential satisfaction, PA, and NA are elaborated upon. Next, the effects for the characteristics of elder vulnerability on residential satisfaction, PA, and NA are given further consideration. Then, interaction effects are discussed. The chapter concludes with suggestions for future research on person-environment interactions.

SUPRAPERSONAL ENVIRONMENT

One hundred and ninety-six (196) urban-dwelling elders were studied to determine the impact of their suprapersonal environment (SPE) on residential satisfaction and subjective well-being. The suprapersonal environment was characterized, in part, by objective and perceived evaluations of neighborhood poverty type. Additionally, the impact of several perceived negative social conditions was also examined.

To briefly reiterate the findings, one SPE characteristic, perceived neighborhood victimization, was predictive of residential satisfaction. One SPE characteristic, perceived neighborhood female-headed households, was predictive of PA. Only one of the six negative social conditions from the SPE, perceived neighborhood unemployment, was predictive of NA. These results indicate, contrary to the hypotheses of the current study, that the SPE does not exert demands on the person, at least not to the extent that we were able to observe corresponding decreases in either residential satisfaction or SWB. There are several possible explanations for this lack of observed effect.

One explanation is that the elders most negatively affected by the SPE that exists in impoverished neighborhoods have already migrated out from those neighborhoods. Census data reveal that there has been a migration of elders from the inner city in the past decade. But reasons for leaving are largely left to speculation, due to lack of follow-up study of these specific migrants from Cleveland. It is plausible that the majority of elders remaining in the inner city may be those who are generally satisfied with their homes and neighborhoods, and/or best able to cope with the SPE of poverty neighborhoods. Therefore, the SPE as specified by the Urban Ecological Model of Aging, is not significant or sufficient enough by itself to evoke residential dissatisfaction and compromised SWB. This explanation suggests that urban elderly who are dissatisfied with their living situation may be able to bring about residential change.

A second possible explanation for the findings has to do with the operationalization of the SPE neighborhood poverty types concepts. Neither objective nor perceived neighborhood poverty type directly affected any of the outcomes of interest. The objective and perceived neighborhood poverty type concepts were based on 1) the percentage of poverty in the neighborhood, and 2) the length of time that level of poverty had existed. When these two variables are used to classify objective neighborhood poverty type, U. S. Census data are used. Consequently, these two variables are likely measured with relative accuracy. However, when these two variables are used to classify perceived neighborhood poverty type, the individuals' perceptions are used. Consequently, it is likely that these two variables are measured with less accuracy. For the perceived measure to have meaning, the level of poverty in the neighborhood must be salient enough to the respondents that they may offer an estimation of its extent. Additionally, the respondents are required to have knowledge of the neighborhood's history of poverty, to enable them to say how long a given level of poverty has existed. This history might be especially difficult to know if the respondent has not been a resident of the neighborhood since 1970 (the most extreme high poverty group has had at least 40% poor since 1970, by definition).

The potential for error in these perceived estimation components may be great, especially for the component dealing with the duration of neighborhood poverty. The data in Table 5 are consistent with the suggestion that such errors in judging neighborhood poverty types may have occurred. Dividing the sample into subsamples based on objective neighborhood poverty type, residents of high poverty areas correctly perceived that their neighborhoods have a poverty level of 40% or more (i.e., the neighborhood is in fact a high poverty one). However, they do not accurately know how long that level of poverty has existed in the neighborhood. In other words, poverty level has personal salience, but the poverty duration aspect of the neighborhood's history is not well known. If the perceived poverty level is used (i.e., without the duration component) to determine neighborhood poverty type, then it is possible that perceived neighborhood poverty type would have an effect on residential satisfaction and SWB.

As a third possible explanation for the failure of the SPE to affect residential satisfaction and SWB, the "reference" neighborhood for the sample of elderly may have been other than the place they resided. In other words, the elders may have had roles they played in neighborhoods outside their neighborhood of residence. Thus, for example, older persons who spend extensive time periods in suburban homes of their children may have used those neighborhoods as their reference group. Further, these roles and associated relationships in other neighborhoods may have been more important to the elders, such that these outside neighborhoods were in fact their reference neighborhoods. If this is the case, it would be more appropriate to study the impact of the SPE of these non-residential reference neighborhoods on residential satisfaction and SWB.

A fourth possible explanation for the failure of the SPE to affect residential satisfaction and SWB concerns the ability of these elders to cope with potentially stressful situations. Subsequent to their competent coping, the negative neighborhood effects may have been diminished. Thus, for example, elders who perceived a high rate of victimization of neighbors in their neighborhood might limit running errands to the early part of the day, when they feel safest. This strategy would minimize the likelihood of them becoming crime victims.

As a fifth explanation for the weak effects of the suprapersonal environment, one may consider alternatives to the Urban Ecological Model of Aging. The reader will recall that the urban model conceptualizes the environment as a source of press, and individuals as having varying levels of ability to manage the presses. An alternative model is Kahana's (1982) congruence model of person-environment interactions. The congruence model looks at the interaction between person and environment as a matching of environment characteristics with personal preferences and needs.   According to this model, goodness-of-fit between person and environment is achieved when the environment characteristics and the individual's preferences and needs are similar. The goodness-of-fit promotes SWB.

Therefore, the Urban Ecological Model of Aging and the congruence model of person-environment interaction are dissimilar. The environment characteristic of age homogeneity provides an example to illustrate the difference. In this example, both models consider the outcome of SWB; however, the urban ecological model focuses on the person's perception of neighborhood age homogeneity. Conversely, the congruence model focuses on the person's preference or need for neighborhood age homogeneity.

Although the congruence model was not developed with personal characteristics of the individual and characteristics of the SPE taken into consideration, the model seems applicable here. Two mechanisms by which the congruence model may relate to the observed findings are 1) inference of needs and preferences from the profile of the SPE; and 2) use of the concept of relative deprivation. The first mechanism is discussed next. The second mechanism will be discussed later, in the section on characteristics of elder vulnerability.

In this study, personal preferences and needs were not assessed, but perhaps they can be inferred by looking at the environmental characteristics that may be resources for elderly living in impoverished neighborhoods. Certainly, such speculation should be followed-up with empirical testing. Examples of impoverished neighborhood resources and matching elder preferences/needs are given below. A good match would promote residential satisfaction and SWB.

In terms of age, the neighborhood characteristic "age heterogeneity" may be matched with the person characteristic "preference to be with a wide range of age groups." This match could provide personal stimulation and involvement with younger people in a variety of roles. Thus, for example, the elderly could serve as surrogate grandparents for neighborhood children. As such, they could baby-sit for working mothers, and offer other means of informal social support.

In terms of race, the neighborhood characteristic "race homogeneity" may be matched with the person characteristic "need to be comfortable in social settings, and to be with others of the same race." This match could reduce fear of the unknown generated by being with others dissimilar to self, and enhance personal comfort during social interaction. It is important to note that this cohort came of age during legalized segregation in this country. Therefore, their social interactions with members of the opposite race were limited. Hence, they would be more comfortable around people like those they grew up with.

With respect to transportation, "collective reliance on public transportation" is characteristic of impoverished neighborhoods, and may be matched with the person characteristic "preference to control one's activity level and mobility." Independence could be promoted by public transportation. Thus, for example, elders could take the bus to the shopping mall to pay bills, make purchases or meet with friends at a time convenient for them. Furthermore, they would not have to wait until their children or someone else had time to take them. The elders would also be able to independently decide when to leave the mall.

With respect to social support, "collective reliance on social support services" is characteristic of impoverished neighborhoods, and may be matched with the person characteristic "need for formal assistance." The formal assistance may allow the elder to remain in the neighborhood, as opposed to relocating to an institutionalized or congregate setting, when faced with increasing frailty. An example of a match in this case is the elder who uses the meals-on-wheels service provided by the neighborhood senior citizens center. The two daily meals brought to the home by center personnel allow the frail elder to cook less often without compromising nutrition. Hence, their children and the elders can feel more comfortable with the decision to remain in the home, despite the present level of frailty.

The last explanation advanced here for the observed weak SPE effects is provided by an optimal discrepancy model of congruence (Kahana, 1982). This model suggests that the environment does not provide for all individual preferences and needs. Therefore, some degree of noncongruence is present, but noncongruence is not inherently bad. If the degree of noncongruence is surmountable, individuals may strive to enhance their competency to reduce the noncongruence and achieve a positive outcome, in this case, residential satisfaction and enhanced SWB. Therefore, in this study, the poverty and negative social conditions may be bothersome, but the elderly individuals strive to put these conditions in proper perspective in terms of the good the neighborhood has to offer (see discussion of neighborhood resources above), in hopes of reducing the noncongruence. The net result of these individual efforts is the observed, mostly statistically nonsignificant, effect of the SPE on residential satisfaction and SWB.

Having discussed the effects of the SPE on residential satisfaction and SWB, the discussion now turns to a consideration of the effects of elder vulnerability characteristics.

CHARACTERISTICS OF ELDER VULNERABILITY

This sample of urban-dwelling elders was studied to determine the impact of characteristics of elder vulnerability on residential satisfaction and subjective well-being. To briefly reiterate the findings regarding these independent variables, the predictors of residential satisfaction are predominately from the domain of elder vulnerability characteristics: perceived social support; received social support; dwelling age; and tenure. Additionally, most of the major predictors of PA are from the domain of elder vulnerability characteristics: sex; income; education; and perceived social support. Likewise, the results further demonstrate that the majority of predictors for NA stem from elder vulnerability characteristics: sex; race; and ADL. There are several possible explanations for these observed effects.

These results, in combination with those regarding the SPE effects, indicate that the elders may be impervious to the SPE (aggregated "people") characteristics because the characteristics of elder vulnerability are of greater importance to them. Elderly persons are more concerned about and influenced by their personal competence in the case of PA and NA, and their immediate dwelling space in the case of NA, and particularly residential satisfaction. Thus, for example, elders who have higher income and education, and who own their own homes have more resources to shelter them from the effects of poverty they see in their neighborhoods. The influence of dwelling characteristics on residential satisfaction has been previously shown in the general literature on residential satisfaction.

A second explanation for the findings concerns the accumulated knowledge regarding elderly residential satisfaction. Research on predictors of residential satisfaction has examined physical characteristics of the environment much more extensively than SPE characteristics. Hence, there is greater guidance in the literature as to which physical environment characteristics to include in models, compared to the guidance for selection of salient SPE characteristics. This point will be further discussed in the section on future research directions.

Kahana's (1982) congruence model provides a third explanation for the greater importance of the elder vulnerability characteristics, versus SPE characteristics, on residential satisfaction and SWB. The reader will recall that goodness-of-fit between person and environment is achieved when the environment characteristics and the individual's preferences and needs are similar. Although, the congruence model was not developed with characteristics of elder vulnerability and SPE taken into consideration, the model seems applicable here. A mechanism by which the congruence model may relate to the observed findings is through use of a related concept, relative deprivation (Diener, 1984).

When personal characteristics are similar to the aggregated characteristics of one's neighbors, it can be said that the two are congruous. Goodness-of-fit exists and SWB is expected to be promoted. In impoverished neighborhoods, the deprivation that exists is experienced across individuals in general, but to different levels. The individuals see that neighbors share the same basic set of circumstances, and any personal deprivation experienced is evaluated relative to that experienced by neighbors. If the individuals conclude that they are no worse off than their neighbors (i.e., the situations are congruous), the individuals suffer no compromised SWB or residential dissatisfaction. Conversely, if they conclude they are worse off (i.e., the situations are noncongruous), SWB may be compromised and residential dissatisfaction experienced. Thus, for example, elders who receive welfare assistance would see themselves as no worse off than their neighbors if they perceive a high rate of welfare assistance in their neighborhood. Therefore, in this case they are not likely to experience relative deprivation.

In addition to the congruence model, a variation of that model, the optimal discrepancy model of congruence (Kahana, 1982) may also be applicable here as a fourth explanation for the current results. The mechanism by which this model operates is also through relative deprivation. In this particular instance, this model would suggest that some degree of noncongruence between personal characteristics and characteristics of one's neighbors exist, but the noncongruence is not inherently bad.

If the individuals perceive themselves to be slightly worse off than their neighbors (i.e., surmountable relative deprivation), they may strive to reduce the discrepancy and achieve a positive outcome (residential satisfaction and enhanced SWB, in this case). An example of discrepancy is the case of elders who are unable to make the necessary repairs to their homes in neighborhoods where properties are well-maintained. Thus, these elders may decide to rent out an extra room, baby-sit or seek formal assistance to finance repairs to the home. Consequently congruence is achieved.

If the individuals perceive themselves to be better off than their neighbors, their appraisals of SWB and residential satisfaction reflect no relative deprivation in the given neighborhood context. If these individuals should move into a non-impoverished neighborhood with an improved SPE, they may then experience relative deprivation, and decreased residential satisfaction and SWB. That is to say, they might then be less well-off when compared to their new more affluent neighbors.

Having discussed the major main effects results obtained by testing the Urban Ecological Model of Aging, the discussion focuses next on possible explanations as to why the interactions predicted by the model were not observed.

INTERACTION EFFECTS

Contrary to expectations, the SPE and selected characteristics of elder vulnerability (i.e., sex, race, marital status, income, physical function/ADL, perceived social support, and received social support) did not interact in their effect on SWB. Thus, the results lead us to reject this operationalization of the environmental docility hypothesis generated by the Urban Ecological Model of Aging. The environmental docility hypothesis asserts that the more competent person is less influenced by environmental factors than a person whose competence is compromised. This suggests, in keeping with the interaction hypothesis set forth in this study, that elderly who have multiple characteristics of vulnerability and thereby experience compromised competence, are in jeopardy. They are at increased risk of being more adversely affected by the perception of social problems reflected in the suprapersonal environment of the inner city.

The resilience of urban-dwelling elders offers one possible explanation for why the current study did not find the predicted interaction. In other words, urban community-dwelling elders appear resilient in the face of their impoverished neighborhoods. The elders are able to muster their resources, as discussed earlier with regards to characteristics of elder vulnerability, thereby minimizing the potential negative effects of the neighborhood.

Hence, the results suggest that the Urban Ecological Model of Aging, based on Lawton and Nahemow's ecological model of aging, may not be an appropriate model to study community-based elders. The ecological model of aging has primarily been applied to frail elders in nursing homes or congregate facilities. Given that personal competence decreases with increased frailty, the ecological model would seem most appropriately applied to these settings. But this study's results indicate a higher level of personal competence among urban community-dwelling elders. Therefore, congruence or resource models of person-environment interactions may be more appropriate to study this population of elders.

FUTURE RESEARCH DIRECTIONS

It was stated at the onset that this study had the potential to make a major contribution to the literature on person-environment interactions. The major contribution was to be the linking of macro (environment) and micro (individual) levels of social scientific theory and analysis. Specifically, it was anticipated that support would be garnered to demonstrate that the SPE is predictive of residential satisfaction and SWB among community-based elders. Of added significance was the use of commensurate perceived versus objective measures of suprapersonal environment characteristics in this study. It is argued in the person-environment fit literature that commensurate objective and perceived measures should be used when examining person-environment interaction.

While the findings offer only very limited support for the idea that the SPE of poor neighborhoods is influential in the lives of urban-dwelling elders, it is premature to conclude that there is no substantive impact. The study results may tell us that it is not easy to identify salient aspects of the SPE that influence the micro-state. The SPE macro-level is very abstract, and the literature does not offer many guidelines as to what characteristics are predictive of which specific micro states. Therefore, at this time, it is somewhat arbitrarily determined which micro-level variable should be chosen as the outcome, and which macro-level SPE variables as the predictors. It may be that different salient macro-level variables are predictive of a particular micro-level outcome.

As other researchers focus on the suprapersonal environment, we should learn more about the SPE and its effects. Delineating the effects of the SPE on elderly SWB is a promising area of research that deserves continued study.

MODELS AND MEASURES

The Urban Ecological Model of Aging should be retained for future research, before a final pronouncement of its inappropriateness for urban community-dwelling elders. Additional testing of the urban ecological model with different samples would add more knowledge to the field. In the present study, most of the elders used the formal support services of the senior citizens centers. This association between the elderly and senior centers may have influenced the current results since social support was predictive of PA and NA. Additionally, these elders may have been less vulnerable to the effects of the SPE variables than would-be respondents who do not have such formal social support networks. Furthermore, future studies should modify how neighborhood poverty type is operationalized. More specifically, preliminary findings of the present study suggest that researchers should use the percent estimation of poverty level in the neighborhood without respect to how long that level of poverty has existed.

Further, congruence models such as those discussed earlier should be reformulated to reflect the SPE and personal characteristics of community-based urban elders, and submitted to empirical test. Then the preferences and/or needs of these elders could be ascertained to test their goodness-of-fit with the SPE, thereby evaluating the appropriateness of the congruence models as currently formulated.

CONCLUSION

In conclusion, this study has contributed knowledge to aid understanding of human social behavior in the context of person-environment interactions. Problems exposed by this study are problems in the field of person-environment interaction theory. These gaps in knowledge require further research.

Bibliography

Alexander, J. & Giesen, B. (1987). From reduction to linkage: The long view of the micro-macro debate. In J. Alexander, B. Giesen, R. Munch, & N. Smelser (Eds.) *The Micro-macro debate* (pp. 1-42). Berkeley: University of California Press.

Andrews, F. & Robinson, J. (1991). Measures of subjective well-being. In J. Robinson, P. Shaver & L. Wrightsman (Eds.) *Measures of personality and social psychological attitudes. Vol. 1* (pp. 61-114). San Diego: Academic Press, Inc.

Atchley, R. C. (1990). Defining the vulnerable older population. In Z. Harel, P. Ehrlich, & R. Hubbard (Eds.) *The vulnerable aged, people, services and policies* (pp. 18-31). New York: Springer Publishing Co., Inc.

Barnes, A. S. (1986). *Black women: Interpersonal relationships in profile–a sociological study of work, home and the community.* Bristol, Indiana: Wyndham Hall Press, Inc.

Biegel, D. & Farkas, K. (1990). The impact of neighborhoods and ethnicity on black and white vulnerable elderly. In Z. Harel, P. Ehrlich & R. Hubbard (Eds.) *The vulnerable aged, people, services and policies* (pp. 116-136). New York: Springer Publishing Co., Inc.

Blau, P. (1987). Contrasting theoretical perspectives. In J. Alexander, B. Giesen, R. Munch, & N. Smelser (Eds.) *The Micro-macro debate* (pp. 71-85). Berkeley: University of California Press.

Brewster, K. L. (1994). Race differences in sexual activity among adolescent women: the role of neighborhood characteristics. *American Sociological Review, 59,* 408-424.

Brown, V. (1995). The effects of poverty environments on elders' subjective well-being: A conceptual model. *The Gerontologist, 35,* 541-548.

Campbell, A., Converse, P. E. & Rodgers, W. L. (1976). *The quality of American life* (pp. 217 - 266). New York: Russell Sage Foundation.

Cantor, M. (1979). The informal support system of New York's inner city elderly: Is ethnicity a factor? In D. Gelfand & A. Kutzik (Eds.) *Ethnicity and aging: Theory, research and policy* (pp. 153-174). New York: Springer Publishing Co., Inc.

Carp, F. M. (1975a). Impact of improved housing on morale and life satisfaction. *The Gerontologist, 15,* 511-515.

——— (1975b). Long-range satisfaction with housing. *The Gerontologist, 15,* 68-72.

——— (1976). Housing and living environments of older people. In R. Binstock & E. Shanas (Eds.) *Handbook of aging and the social sciences* (pp. 244-271). New York: Van Nostrand Reinhold.

——— (1979). Ego defense or cognitive consistency effects of environmental evaluation. *Journal of Gerontology, 30,* 707-716.

——— (1983). A complementary/congruence model of well-being or mental health for the community elderly. In I. Altmen, J. Wohlwill & M. P. Lawton (Eds.) *The elderly and the physical environment.* New York: Plenum.

Carp, F. M. & Christensen, D. (1986). Technical environmental assessment predictors of residential satisfaction. *Research on Aging, 8,* 269-287.

Cohen, S., Mermelstein, R., Kamarck, T. & Hoberman, H. M. (1985). Measuring the functional components of social support. In I. G. Sarason & B. R. Sarason (Eds.) *Social support: Theory, research and applications* (pp. 73-94). Dordrecht, Netherlands: Martinus Nijhoff.

Coleman, J. (1987). Microfoundations and macrosocial behavior. In J. Alexander, B. Giesen, R. Munch, & N. Smelser (Eds.) *The Micro-macro debate* (pp. 153-173). Berkeley: University of California Press.

Conner, K. A. (1992). *Aging America: Issues facing an aging society.* Englewood Cliffs, N.J.: Prentice Hall.

Coulton, C., Chow, J. & Panday, S. (1990). *An analysis of poverty and related conditions in Cleveland area neighborhoods.* Cleveland: Mandel School of Applied Social Sciences, Case Western Reserve University.

Coulton, C., Chow, J. & Sering, M. (1991). *Resources and capacities in Cleveland's low-income neighborhoods.* Cleveland: Mandel School of Applied Social Sciences, Case Western Reserve University.

Crane, J. (1991). The epidemic theory of ghettos and neighborhood effects on dropping out and teenage childbearing. *American Journal of Sociology, 96,* 1226-1259.

Danziger, S., Jakubson, G., Schwartz, S. & Smolensky, E. (1982). Work and welfare as determinants of female poverty and household headship. *Quarterly Journal of Economics, 97,* 519-534.

Diener, E. (1984). Subjective well-being. *Psychological Bulletin, 95,* 542-575.

Diener, E., Emmons, R. A., Larsen, R. J., & Griffin, S. (1985). The satisfaction with life scale. *Journal of Personality Assessment, 49,* 71 - 75.

Dowd, J. & Bengston, V. (1978). Aging in minority populations: An examination of the double jeopardy hypothesis. *Journal of Gerontology, 33,* 427-436.

Duke University Center for the Study of Aging and Human Development (1978). *Multidimensional functional assessment: The OARS Methodology.* Durham, N.C.: Duke University.

Dunkel-Schetter, C. & Bennett, T. (1990). Differentiating the cognitive and behavioral aspects of social support. In I. G. Sarason & B. R. Sarason (Eds.) *Social support: Theory, research and applications* (pp. 267-296). Dordrecht, Netherlands: Martinus Nijhoff.

Eggebeen, D. L. & Lichter, D. T. (1991). Race, family structure, and changing poverty among American children. *American Sociological Review, 56,* 801-817.

Ford, A. B., Haug, M. R., Jones, P. K., Roy, A. W. & Folmar, S. J. (1990). Race-related differences among elderly urban residents: A Cohort study, 1975-1984. *Journal of Gerontology, 45,* S164-171.

Galster, G. & Hesser, G. (1981). Residential satisfaction: Compositional and contextual correlates. *Environment and Behavior, 13,* 735 -758.

Gerstein, D. (1987). To unpack micro and macro: Link small with large and part with whole. In J. Alexander, B. Giesen, R. Munch & N. Smelser (Eds.) *The Micro-macro debate* (pp. 86-111). Berkeley: University of California Press.

Gibson, R. (1986, Winter). Blacks in an aging society [Special issue]. *Daedalus,* "The Aging society", 349-372.

─── (1989). Minority aging research: Opportunity and challenge. *Journal of Gerontology: Social Sciences, 44,* S2-S3.

Golant, S. (1982). Individual differences underlying the dwelling satisfaction of the elderly. *Journal of Social Issues, 38,* 121-133.

Harel, Z., Ehrlich, P. & Hubbard, R. (Eds.). (1990). *The vulnerable aged, people, services and policies.* New York: Springer Publishing Co., Inc.

Havighurst, R., Neugarten, B. & Tobin, S. (1961). The measurement of life satisfaction. *Journal of Gerontology, 16,* 134-143.

Inner-city pirates. (1991, November 10). *The Cleveland Plain Dealer,* p. 2-C.

Jackson, M., Kolody, B. & Wood, J. (1982). To be old and black: The case for double jeopardy on income and health. In R. Manuel (Ed.) *Minority aging: Sociological and social psychological issues,* (pp. 77-82). Westport, Conn: Greenwood Press.

Jackson, J., Bacon, J. & Peterson, J. (1977). Life satisfaction among black urban elderly. *Aging and Human Development, 8,* 169-179.

Jackson, M. & Wood, J. (1976). *Aging in America: Implications for the Black aged.* Washington, D.C.: National Council on Aging.

Jasso, G. (1988). Principles of theoretical analysis. *Sociological Theory, 6,* 1-20.

Jaynes, G. & Williams, Jr., R. (1991). A common destiny: Blacks and American society. In N. Yetman (Ed.) *Majority and minority: The dynamics of race and ethnicity in American life* (5th Ed.) (pp. 477-497). Boston: Allyn and Bacon. (Reprinted from *A common destiny: Blacks and American society,* 1989).

Jirovec, R., Jirovec, M. & Bosse, R. (1985). Residential satisfaction as a function of micro and macro environmental conditions among urban elderly men. *Research on Aging, 7,* 607-616.

Kane, R. A. & Kane, R. L. (1981). *Assessing the elderly.* Lexington, MA: Lexington Books.

Kahana, E. (1982). A congruence model of person-environment interaction. In M. P. Lawton, P. G. Windley & T. O. Byerts (Eds.) *Aging and the environment: Theoretical approaches* (pp. 97-121). New York: Springer Publishing Co., Inc.

Kahana, E., Kahana, B. & Kinney, J. (1990). Coping among vulnerable elders. In Z. Harel, P. Ehrlich & R. Hubbard (Eds.) *The vulnerable aged: People, services and policies* (pp. 64-85). New York: Springer Publishing Co., Inc.

Kercher, K. (1992). Assessing subjective well-being in the old-old: The PANAS as a measure of orthogonal dimensions of positive and negative affect. *Research on Aging, 14,* 131-168.

Krause, N. (1987). Chronic financial strain, social support, and depressive symptoms among older adults. *Psychology and Aging, 2,* 185 - 192.

Larson, R. (1978). Thirty years of research on the subjective well-being of older Americans. *Journal of Gerontology, 33,* 109-125.

Lawton, M. P. (1980a). *Environment and aging.* Monterey, Calif.: Brooks/Cole Publishing Co.

———— (1980b). Housing the elderly: Residential quality and residential satisfaction among the elderly. *Research on Aging,* 2,309-328.

———— (1985). Housing and living environments of older people. In R. H. Binstock & E. Shanas (Eds.) *Handbook on aging and the social sciences* (pp. 450-478). New York: Van Nostrand Reinhold Co.

———— (1990). Vulnerability and socioenvironmental factors. In Z. Harel, P. Ehrlich & R. Hubbard (Eds.) *The vulnerable aged: People, services and policies* (pp. 104-115). New York: Springer Publishing Co., Inc.

Lawton, M. P., Brody, E. M. & Turner-Massey, P. (1978). The relationships of environmental factors to changes in well-being. *The Gerontologist, 18,* 133-137.

Lawton, M. P. & Hoover, S. L. (1979). *Housing and neighborhood: Objective and subjective quality.* Philadelphia: Philadelphia Geriatric Center.

Lawton, M. P., Kleban, M. & Carlson, D. (1973). The inner-city resident: To move or not to move. *The Gerontologist, 13,* 443-448.

Lawton, M. P., Moss, M. & Moles, E. (1984). The suprapersonal neighborhood context of older people: Age heterogeneity and well-being. *Environment and Behavior, 16,* 89-109.

Lawton, M. P. & Nahemow, L. (1979). Social areas and the well-being of tenants in housing for the elderly. *Multivariate Behavioral Research, 14,* 463-484.

Lawton, M. P. & Nahemow, L. (1973). Ecology and the aging process. In C. Eisdorfer & M. P. Lawton (Eds.) *Psychology of adult development and aging* (pp. 619-674). Washington, DC: American Psychological Association.

Lawton, M. P. & Simon, B. (1968). The ecology of social relationships in housing for the elderly. *Gerontologist, 8,* 108-115.

Lawton, M. P., Windley, P. G. & Byerts, T. O. (Eds.) (1982). *Aging and the environment: Theoretical approaches*. New York: Springer Publishing Co., Inc.

Lewis, O. (1966). *La Vida*. New York: Random House, Inc.

Liang, J. & Whitelaw, N. (1990). Assessing the physical and mental health of the elderly. In S. Stahl (Ed.) *The legacy of longevity: Health and health care in later life* (pp. 35-54). Newbury Park, CA: SAGE Publications, Inc.

Lubben, J. E., & Becerra, R. M. (1987). Social support among Black, Mexican and Chinese elderly. In D. Gelfand & C. Barresi (Eds.) *Ethnic dimensions of aging* (pp. 130-144). New York: Springer Publishing Co., Inc.

Lynn, Jr., L. E. & McGeary, M. G. (Eds.) (1990). *Inner-city poverty in the United States*. Washington, D.C.: National Academy Press.

Markides, K. S., Liang, J. & Jackson, J. S. (1990). Race, ethnicity and aging: Conceptual and methodological issues. In R. H. Binstock and L. K. George (Eds.) *Handbook of aging and the social sciences*, (3rd ed.) (pp. 362-381). Boston: Academic Press, Inc.

Markides, K. & Mindel, C. (1987). *Aging & ethnicity*, "Mental health and psychological well-being," 121-147. Beverly Hills: Sage Publications.

Massey, D. (1990). American apartheid: Segregation and the making of the underclass. *American Journal of Sociology, 96,* 329-357.

Massey, D. & Denton, N. (1991). Trends in the residential segregation Blacks, Hispanics, and Asians: 1970-1980. In N. Yetman (Ed.) *Majority and minority: The dynamics of race and ethnicity in American life*, (5th ed.) (pp. 352-378). Boston: Allyn and Bacon. (Reprinted from *American Sociological Review*, 1987, *52*.)

Massey, D. & Denton, N. (1993). *American apartheid: Segregation and the making of the underclass*. Cambridge: Harvard University Press.

Massey, D. & Eggers, M. (1990). The ecology of inequality: Minorities and the concentration of poverty, 1970-1980. *American Journal of Sociology, 95,* 1153-1188.

McAdoo, J. (1979). Well-being and fear of crime among the black elderly. In D. Gelfand & A. Kutzik (Eds.) *Ethnicity and aging. Theory, research and policy*, (pp. 277-290). New York: Springer Publishing Co., Inc.

McAdoo, J. L. (1983). Fear of crime and victimization: Black residents in a high-risk urban environment. In R. McNelly & J. Colen (Eds.) *Aging in minority groups*, 153-160. Beverly Hills: Sage Publications.

McNeely, R. L. (1983). Race, sex and victimization of the elderly. In R. McNelly & J. Colen (Eds.) *Aging in minority groups*, (pp. 137-152). Beverly Hills: Sage Publications.

Miethe, R. & McDowall, D. (1993). Contextual effects in models of criminal victimization. *Social Forces, 71*, 741-759.

Morris, E., Crull, S. & Winter, M. (1976). Housing norms, housing satisfaction and the propensity to move. *J Marriage and the Family, 38*, 309-320.

Myers, P. (1978). *Neighborhood conservation and the elderly*. Washington, D.C.: The Conservation Foundation.

Northern Ohio Data & Information Service (1991a). *1990 Street address/census tract guide Cuyahoga county*. Cleveland: Cleveland State University.

Northern Ohio Data & Information Service (1991b). *1990 Census tract/BNA boundary delineations, City of Cleveland, Cuyahoga County*. Cleveland: Cleveland State University.

Norusis, M. J./SPSS Inc. (1990). *SPSS/PC+ Statistics 4.0*. Chicago: SPSS Inc.

Palmer, J., Smeeding, T., & Jencks, C. (1988). The uses and limits of income comparisons. In J. L. Palmer, T. Smeeding & B. Torrey (Eds.) *The vulnerable* (pp. 9-28), Washington, D.C.: The Urban Institute Press.

Rodgers, Jr., H. (1996). *Poor women, poor children: American poverty in the 1990s* (3rd ed.). Armonk, New York: M.E. Sharpe.

Rosenberg, M. (1965). *Society and the adolescent self-image*. Princeton, N. J.: Princeton University Press.

Rosow, I. (1967). *Social integration of the aged*. New York: Free-Press.

Schaie, K., Orchowsky, S. & Parham, I. (1982). Measuring age and sociocultural change: The case of race and life satisfaction. In R. Manuel (Ed.) *Minority aging: Sociological and social psychological issues* (pp. 223-230). Westport, Conn: Greenwood Press.

Schiller, B. R. (1989). *The Economics of poverty & discrimination.* Englewood Cliffs, N.J.: Prentice Hall.

Smeeding, T. M. (1990). Economic status of the elderly. In R. H. Binstock & L. K. George (Eds.) *Handbook of aging and the social sciences* (3rd ed.) (pp. 362-381). Boston: Academic Press, Inc.

Siu, A., Reuben, D., and Hays, R. (1990). Hierarchical measures of physical function in ambulatory geriatrics. *Journal of the American Geriatric Society, 38,* 1113 - 1119.

Stack, C. B. (1974). *All our kin.* New York: Harper & Row, Publishers.

Tally, T. A. & Kaplan, J. (1956). The Negro aged. *Gerontological Newsletter, 3.*

Tate, N. (1983). The Black aging experience. In R. McNelly & J. Colen (Eds.) *Aging in minority groups,* (pp. 95-107). Beverly Hills: Sage Publications.

Tienda, M. & Jensen, L. (1988). Poverty and minorities: A quarter-century profile of color and socioeconomic disadvantage. In G. Sandefur and M. Tienda (Eds.) *Divided opportunities: Minorities, poverty and social policy (pp. 23-61).* New York: Plenum Press.

Torres-Gil, F. (1986, Winter). The Latinization of a multigenerational population: Hispanics in an aging society. *Daedalus,* [Special issue]. 325-348.

Varghese, R. & Medinger, F. (1979). Fatalism in response to stress among the minority aged. In D. Gelfand & A. Kutzik, *Ethnicity and aging: Theory, research and policy,* (pp. 96-116). New York: Springer Publishing Co., Inc.

Wacquant, L. & Wilson, W. J. (1989). The cost of racial and class exclusion in the inner city. In N. Yetman (Ed.) *Majority and minority: The dynamics of race and ethnicity in American life* (5th ed.) (pp. 498-522). Boston: Allyn and Bacon. (Reprinted from *The Annuals of the American Academy of Political and Social Science,* 1989, *501).*

Ward, R. A. (1977). The impact of subjective age and stigma on older persons. *Journal of Gerontology, 32,* 227-32.

————— (1983). The stability of racial differences across age strata. *Sociology and social research, 67,* 312-323.

Ward, R., LaGory, M. & Sherman, S. (1985). Neighborhood and network age concentration: Does age homogeneity matter for older people? *Social Psychology Quarterly, 48,* 138-149.

Watson, D., Clark, L. A., & Tellegen, A. (1988). Development and validation of brief measures of positive and negative affect: The PANAS scales. *Journal of Personality and Social Psychology, 54*, 1063 - 1070.

Watson, W. H. (1983). Selected demographic and social aspects of older blacks. In R. McNelly & J. Colen (Eds.) *Aging in minority groups* (pp. 42-49). Beverly Hills: Sage Publications.

Wethington, E. & Kessler, R. (1986). Perceived support, received support, and adjustment to stressful life events. *Journal of Health and Social Behavior, 27,*
78-89.

Wilson, W. J. (1987) *The Truly disadvantaged.* Chicago: The University of Chicago Press.

Windley, P., Byerts, T., & Ernst, F. (Eds.). (1975). *Theory development in environment and aging.* Washington, D.C.: Gerontological Society.

Wiseman, R. F. (1980). Why older people move: Theoretical issues. *Research on Aging, 2*, 141-154.

Zinn, M. (1991). Family, race, and poverty in the eighties. In N. Yetman (Ed.) *Majority and minority: The dynamics of race and ethnicity in American life*, (pp. 512-522). Boston: Allyn and Bacon. (Reprinted from *Signs, 14*).

APPENDIX A
QUESTIONNAIRE

TIME BEGAN _____   TIME END _____   TOTAL TIME _____

Hello, my name is Valerie Brown and I am completing my PhD in sociology at Case Western Reserve University. I am also a registered nurse. I am doing a study of older people in the City of Cleveland. I am interested in measuring how older people, like you, feel about their homes, neighborhoods and life in general. This study could help to design programs to make life better for older Americans living in large cities. I would like you to answer a short questionnaire. It will take about 15 minutes or so. I will not use your name or any personal information to identify you in my study results. All of your answers are private and confidential. If you complete the questionnaire, you will be paid $10.00 for your time. Will you please take a few minutes and answer some questions for me? The first question is

LANGUAGE   What language do you speak most of the time?

        1 English

        0 other

[IF ANSWER IS OTHER THAN ENGLISH, SAY "AT THIS TIME I AM INTERVIEWING PEOPLE WHO SPEAK ENGLISH MOST OF THE TIME. IN THE FUTURE I HOPE TO INTERVIEW PEOPLE WHO SPEAK A LANGUAGE OTHER THAN ENGLISH MOST OF THE TIME. THANK YOU FOR YOUR TIME. BYE."]

I. PERSONAL CHARACTERISTICS OF VULNERABILITY

A. Demographics

AGE   1.   What is your date of birth? [SUBJECT MUST BE BORN NO
              LATER THAN 9/1/31 (60 YEARS OR OLDER)]

              mo._____ day___ year____   _____ AGE

SEX   2. What is your sex?

                  0 male
                  1 female

RACE   3. What is your race?

                  0 white or Euro-American, non-Hispanic
                  1 black or African-American, non-Hispanic
                  2 Asian
                  3 Hispanic
                  - other (specify) _____

           [IF PERSON IS NOT BLACK OR WHITE SAY "AT THIS TIME I AM
           INTERVIEWING PEOPLE WHO ARE BLACK OR WHITE. IN THE
           FUTURE I HOPE TO INTERVIEW PEOPLE WHO ARE OTHER THAN
           BLACK OR WHITE THANK YOU FOR YOUR TIME. BYE."]

MSTATUS1   4. Are you presently

                  1 single (never married) [iF NEVER MARRIED SKIP #5]
                  2 married
                  3 divorced
                  4 separated
                  5 widowed
                  - Not answered

MSTATUS2   5. How long have you been

                  _____ (marital status from
                  above) _____

                  - Not answered

EDUC   6. What level of education have you completed?

                  1 less than 4th grade
                  2 5th - 8th grade
                  3 9th - 11th grade
                  4 high school
                  5 some college
                  6 college graduate (Bachelor's degree)
                  7 college graduate (Master's degree)
                  - Not answered

              I B. Perceived health related measures

HEALTH1   7. Would you rate your overall health at the present time
           as

                  4 excellent
                  3 very good
                  2 good
                  1 fair
                  0 poor
                  - Not answered

Now I'd like to ask you some questions about how much difficulty you have doing certain activities.

How much difficulty do you have:

ADL1   8. Doing strenuous physical activities, like hiking, tennis, bicycling, jogging, and swimming?

    1 None
    2 A little
    3 Some
    4 Quite a bit
    5 Very much
    - Not answered

ADL2   9. Doing heavy work around the house, like washing windows, walls, or floor?

    1 None
    2 A little
    3 Some
    4 Quite a bit
    5 Very much
    - Not answered

ADL3   10. Going shopping for groceries or clothes?

    1 None
    2 A little
    3 Some
    4 Quite a bit
    5 Very much
    - Not answered

ADL4   11. Getting to places out of walking distance?

    1 None
    2 A little
    3 Some
    4 Quite a bit
    5 Very much
    - Not answered

ADL5   12. Bathing, either a sponge bath, tub bath, or shower?

    1 None
    2 A little
    3 Some
    4 Quite a bit
    5 Very much
    - Not answered

ADL6   13. Dressing, like putting on a shirt, buttoning and zipping, or putting on shoes?

         1 None
         2 A little
         3 Some
         4 Quite a bit
         5 Very much
         - Not answered

I A. Demographics

WORK   14. Are you currently [CHECK ALL THAT APPLY]

         ____ 1 retired
         ____ 2 disabled
         ____ 3 working full-time
         ____ 4 working part-time
         ____ 5 housewife
         ____ -Not answered

TENURE   15. Is your home

         2 owned by you
         1 rented by you
         0 other arrangement (specify) _____
         - Not answered

HSEHLDSZ   16. How many people live with you?_____

         [IF NONE SKIP QUESTIONS #17-19 GO TO #20]

         - Not answered

RELATIVES   17. What is each person's age and relationship to you?

         AGE   RELATIONSHIP

         ____   _____
         ____   _____
         ____   _____
         ____   _____
         ____   _____
         ____   _____
         ____   _____
         ____   _____

HEADHSE   18. Who is the head of the household? [ASK IF NOT LIVING ALONE]

    1 self
    0 other, specify _____
    - Not answered

MOVEIN   19. Of the people in your household, did any of them move in with you? [ASK IF NOT LIVING ALONE]

    0 No, I moved in with them
    1 Yes, specify _____
    - Other, specify _____

DWELTYPE   20. Do you live in a(n)

    3 single- family house
    2 part of a two-family house
    1 apartment
    0 other (specify) _____
    - Not answered

DWELSIZE   21. How many rooms do you have in your house or apartment? Please include only finished and furnished rooms and do not count hallways and bathrooms_____

    - Not answered

NOBATHS   22. How many bathrooms?_____

    - Not answered

LRESID   23. How long have you lived in your present home?

    _____(months, if less than 1 year)

    _____ years

    - Not answered

NSAT1   24. To what extent do you feel your present neighborhood is a good place for you (and your family) to live?

    1 Not at all
    2 A little
    3 Somewhat
    4 Quite a bit
    5 Very much
    - Not answered

HSAT1   25. How satisfied are you with your present _house or apartment_ as a place to live?

          1 Not at all
          2 A little
          3 Somewhat
          4 Quite a bit
          5 Very much
          - Not answered

               I C. Perceived and received social support

The next few questions are about you helping others and them helping you.

To what extent do you agree or disagree with the following statements

SUPPORT1   26. These days I really don't know who I can count on for help

          1 Strongly agree
          2 Agree
          3 Neither agree nor disagree
          4 Disagree
          5 Strongly disagree
          - Not answered

SUPPORT2   27. When I need suggestions for how to deal with a personal problem I know there is someone I can turn to.

          1 Strongly agree
          2 Agree
          3 Neither agree nor disagree
          4 Disagree
          5 Strongly disagree
          - Not answered

SUPPORT3   28: There are several different people with whom I enjoy spending time.

          1 Strongly agree
          2 Agree
          3 Neither agree nor disagree
          4 Disagree
          5 Strongly disagree
          - Not answered

SUPPORT4   29. If I needed some help in moving to a new home, I would have a hard time finding someone to help me.

          1 Strongly agree
          2 Agree
          3 Neither agree nor disagree
          4 Disagree
          5 Strongly disagree
          - Not answered

SUPPORT5   30. If I were sick, there would be almost no one I could
                find to help me with my daily chores.

                    1 Strongly agree
                    2 Agree
                    3 Neither agree nor disagree
                    4 Disagree
                    5 Strongly disagree
                    - Not answered

SUPPORT6   31. Most people I know think highly of me.

                    1 Strongly agree
                    2 Agree
                    3 Neither agree nor disagree
                    4 Disagree
                    5 Strongly disagree
                    - Not answered

Now I'd like you to think back over the past year and tell me

In the last year how often has someone [FOR QUESTIONS #30 - 38]

SUPPORT7   32. Watched after your possessions while you were away?

                    1 never
                    2 once in a while
                    3 fairly often
                    4 very often
                    - Not answered

SUPPORT8   33. Loaned or given you something (a physical object
                other than money) that you needed?

                    1 never
                    2 once in a while
                    3 fairly often
                    4 very often
                    - Not answered

SUPPORT9   34. Pitched in to help you do something that needed to
                get done, like household chores or yardwork?

                    1 never
                    2 once in a while
                    3 fairly often
                    4 very often
                    - Not answered

SUPPORT10   35. Been right there with you (physically) in a
                stressful situation?

                    1 never
                    2 once in a while
                    3 fairly often
                    4 very often
                    - Not answered

SUPPORT11   36. Listened to you talk about your private feelings?

                      1 never
                      2 once in a while
                      3 fairly often
                      4 very often
                      - Not answered

In the past year how often has someone

SUPPORT12   37. Talked over their problems and private feelings with
                 you?

                      1 never
                      2 once in a while
                      3 fairly often
                      4 very often
                      - Not answered

SUPPORT13   38. Depended on you for something they needed (a
                 physical object other than money)?

                      1 never
                      2 once in a while
                      3 fairly often
                      4 very often
                      - Not answered

                      I D. Self-Esteem

For the following statements tell me if you strongly agree, agree,
neither agree nor disagree, disagree, or strongly disagree.

ESTEEM1   39. I feel that I'm a person of worth, at least on an
                 equal plane with others.

                      1 Strongly agree
                      2 Agree
                      3 Neither agree nor disagree
                      4 Disagree
                      5 Strongly disagree
                      - Not answered

ESTEEM2   40. I feel I do not have much to be proud of.

                      1 Strongly agree
                      2 Agree
                      3 Neither agree nor disagree
                      4 Disagree
                      5 Strongly disagree
                      - Not answered

ESTEEM3   41. I wish I could have more respect for myself.

         1 Strongly agree
         2 Agree
         3 Neither agree nor disagree
         4 Disagree
         5 Strongly disagree
         - Not answered

ESTEEM4   42. I certainly feel useless at times.

         1 Strongly agree
         2 Agree
         3 Neither agree nor disagree
         4 Disagree
         5 Strongly disagree
         - Not answered

HEALTH2   43. My physical health compared to most people my age is
             poor

         1 Strongly agree
         2 Agree
         3 Neither agree nor disagree
         4 Disagree
         5 Strongly disagree
         - Not answered

         I E. Dwelling characteristics

Now for some questions about your home.

DWELLING   44. How old would you say your house or apartment is?
AGE

         1   less than 1 year
         2   1 - 5 years
         3   6 - 10 years
         4   11 -20 years
         5   21 - 30 years
         6   30 years or older
         - Not answered

CMHA   45. Do you live in a Cuyahoga Metropolitan Housing
             Authority (CMHA) housing project?

         1 yes
         0 no
         - Not answered

SUBSIDY   46. Is part of your mortgage or rent paid by the federal
               government?

                    1 yes
                    0 no
                    - Not answered

DMOVE1   47. How much do you agree or disagree with this
               statement: At the present time, I have no desire to
               move from where I'm currently living

                    1 Strongly agree
                    2 Agree
                    3 Neither agree nor disagree
                    4 Disagree
                    5 Strongly Disagree
                    - Not answered

II. SUPRAPERSONAL ENVIRONMENTAL CHARACTERISTICS

A. Extent and Duration of Poverty

Now I would like to ask you some questions about the neighborhood
you live in. For these questions please think of your neighborhood
as being bordered by _____ at the North, _____ at the
East, _____ at the South, and _____ at the West.

POVEXTENT   48. What percentage of the people in your neighborhood
                do you think are poor?_____

                    - Not answered

POVDUR   49. Have these people become poor within:

                    1 the past ten years
                    2 the past eleven to twenty years
                    3 the past twenty-one years or longer
                    - Not answered

II B. Negative social conditions in the neighborhood

DELINQU   50. What percentage of the youths in your neighborhood do
                you think have been charged with juvenile
                delinquency? _____%

VICTIM   51. What percentage of the people in your neighborhood do
                you think have been a victim of a serious crime?_____%

JOBLESS   52. What percentage of the adults in your neighborhood do
                you think are not working but are actively looking
                for work?_____%

90

FEMHEAD 53. What percentage of children in your neighborhood do you think have only one parent, the mother, present in the home?_____%

WELFARE 54. What percentage of the adults in your neighborhood do you think receive welfare assistance from the government?_____%

TEENPREG 55. What percentage of female teenagers in your neighborhood do you think had a baby last year?_____%

AGEMIX 56. Which age groups would you say are the 3 largest in your neighborhood? [PAUSE FOR RESPONSE] What is the order of these 3 age groups from largest to smallest?

(Rankings)

___ 0 children: infant to 12 years old _____
___ 1 teenagers: 13 - 19 years old _____
___ 2 young adults: 20 - 40 years old _____
___ 3 middle adults: 41 - 64 years old _____
___ 4 older adults: 65 and older _____

Now I'd like to ask a few questions about crime.

FEARCR 57. Tell me to what extent are you afraid of crime in your neighborhood?

1 Not at all
2 A little
3 Somewhat
4 Quite a bit
5 Very much
- Not answered

VICRIME 58. Have you ever been a victim of a crime

1 Yes
0 No [SKIP QUESTIONS #59 - 62 GO TO #63]
- Not answered

VICFREQ 59. If yes, how many times?_____

CRIMTYPE 60. What was the crime(s)?

(1) _____

(2) _____

(3) _____

CRIMTIME   61.   When and where did the crime(s) happen?

(1) _____ (year)   _____ place

(2) _____ (year)   _____ place

(3) _____ (year)   _____ place

CRIMELOC   62.   Did the crime occur in your present neighborhood?

1 Yes
0 No
- Not answered

NRACE   63.   Is your neighborhood

1 all white
2 mostly white
3 half white and half black
4 mostly black
5 all black
-other (specify)
- Not answered

II C. Negative housing conditions in the neighborhood

How much do you agree or disagree with the following statements:

HQUALITY   64. I rate the quality of the houses in my neighborhood as generally good

        1 Strongly agree
        2 Agree
        3 Neither agree nor disagree
        4 Disagree
        5 Strongly Disagree
        - Not answered

APTQUAL   65. I rate the quality of the apartment buildings in my neighborhood as generally good

        1 Strongly agree
        2 Agree
        3 Neither agree nor disagree
        4 Disagree
        5 Strongly Disagree
        - Not answered

III. NEIGHBORHOOD SATISFACTION

NSAT2   66. I am dissatisfied with my neighborhood as a place to live

        1 Strongly agree
        2 Agree
        3 Neither agree nor disagree
        4 Disagree
        5 Strongly Disagree
        - Not answered

IV. HOUSING SATISFACTION

HSAT2   67. I am dissatisfied with my house or apartment

        1 Strongly agree
        2 Agree
        3 Neither agree nor disagree
        4 Disagree
        5 Strongly Disagree
        - Not answered

HSEMAINT   68. To what extent do you feel the houses and apartments
                 your neighborhood are well-kept up

                     1 Not at all
                     2 A little
                     3 Somewhat
                     4 Quite a bit
                     5 Very much
                     - Not answered

V. DESIRE TO MOVE

DMOVE2   69. How much do you want to move at this time

                     1 Not at all
                     2 A little
                     3 Somewhat
                     4 Quite a bit
                     5 Very much
                     - Not answered

VI. PSYCHOLOGICAL WELL-BEING

A. Positive and negative affect

Tell me to what extent you have felt this way in the past two months
[QUESTIONS # 70 - 75]

PA1   70.   Excited

                     1 Not at all
                     2 A little
                     3 Somewhat
                     4 Quite a bit
                     5 Very much
                     - Not answered

PA2   71.   Enthusiastic

                     1 Not at all
                     2 A little
                     3 Somewhat
                     4 Quite a bit
                     5 Very much
                     - Not answered

NA1   72.   Distressed

                     1 Not at all
                     2 A little
                     3 Somewhat
                     4 Quite a bit
                     5 Very much
                     - Not answered

NA2 73.   Upset

          1 Not at all
          2 A little
          3 Somewhat
          4 Quite a bit
          5 Very much
          - Not answered

PA3 74.   Alert

          1 Not at all
          2 A little
          3 Somewhat
          4 Quite a bit
          5 Very much
          - Not answered

NA3 75.   Scared

          1 Not at all
          2 A little
          3 Somewhat
          4 Quite a bit
          5 Very much
          - Not answered

For each of the following statements tell me how much you agree or
disagree with the statement

PA4 76.   In the past 2 months I have felt inspired

          1 Strongly agree
          2 Agree
          3 Neither agree nor disagree
          4 Disagree
          5 Strongly Disagree
          - Not answered

PA5 77.   In the past 2 months I have felt determined

          1 Strongly agree
          2 Agree
          3 Neither agree nor disagree
          4 Disagree
          5 Strongly Disagree
          - Not answered

NA4 78.   In the past 2 months I have felt nervous

          1 Strongly agree
          2 Agree
          3 Neither agree nor disagree
          4 Disagree
          5 Strongly Disagree
          - Not answered

NA5   79.   In the past 2 months I have felt afraid

                        1 Strongly agree
                        2 Agree
                        3 Neither agree nor disagree
                        4 Disagree
                        5 Strongly Disagree
                        - Not answered

NA6   80.   In the past 2 months I have felt irritable

                        1 Strongly agree
                        2 Agree
                        3 Neither agree nor disagree
                        4 Disagree
                        5 Strongly Disagree
                        - Not answered

PA6   81.   In the past 2 months I have felt strong

                        1 Strongly agree
                        2 Agree
                        3 Neither agree nor disagree
                        4 Disagree
                        5 Strongly Disagree
                        - Not answered

                    VI C. Satisfaction With Life

LIFESAT1   82.   So far, I feel that I have gotten the important things
                   want in life

                        1 Strongly agree
                        2 Agree
                        3 Neither agree nor disagree
                        4 Disagree
                        5 Strongly Disagree
                        - Not answered

LIFESAT2   83.   The conditions of my life are excellent

                        1 Strongly agree
                        2 Agree
                        3 Neither agree nor disagree
                        4 Disagree
                        5 Strongly Disagree
                        - Not answered

LIFESAT3   84.   If I could live my life over, I would change almost
                   nothing

                        1 Strongly agree
                        2 Agree
                        3 Neither agree nor disagree
                        4 Disagree
                        5 Strongly Disagree
                        - Not answered

Now for the last few questions.

LIFESAT4   85.   To what extent is your life close to your ideal

                        1 Not at all
                        2 A little
                        3 Somewhat
                        4 Quite a bit
                        5 Very much
                        - Not answered

LIFESAT5   86.   To what extent are you satisfied with your life

                        1 Not at all
                        2 A little
                        3 Somewhat
                        4 Quite a bit
                        5 Very much
                        - Not answered

I A. Demographics

HEALTH3   87.   Tell me, in general do you consider yourself to be:

                        1 a very healthy person
                        2 a healthy person
                        3 a fairly healthy person
                        4 a sick person
                        5 a very sick person
                        - Not answered

CHILNEAR   88.   Do you have any adult children who live near by?

                        1 yes
                        0 no [SKIP QUESTION #89]

CHILCLSE   89.   How close is the nearest adult child?

                        0 live with me
                        1 less than 10 miles away
                        2 11 to 20 miles away
                        3 21 miles or more away

Now for the last question.

INCOME1   90.   For the year 1991, did you receive income from the
                  following sources? [CHECK ALL THAT APPLY]

                        ____1 social security retirement
                        ____2 social security disability
                        ____3 full-time employment
                        ____4 part-time employment
                        ____5 welfare
                        ____6 private pension
                        ____7 other (specify)_____
                        ____-Not answered

97

INCOME2   91. For the year 1990, what was your income from all
                sources?_____

IF REFUSES TO ANSWER THIS QUESTION SAY, " IF NOT THE ACTUAL DOLLAR
AMOUNT THEN TELL ME IN WHICH OF THE FOLLOWING CATEGORIES WOULD YOU
FALL?"

                    0 less than or equal to $2500
                    1 $2501 - 5,000
                    2 $5,001 - 10,000
                    3 $10,001 - 15,000
                    4 $15,001 - 25,000
                    5 $25,001 or more
                    - Not answered

That's the end of the interview. Thank you for participating in this
study. To show my appreciation for your time I would like to send you
a check for $10.00. To what address should I send the check?

             STREET _____

             APARTMENT_____

             CITY_____

             STATE AND ZIP_____

             PHONE_____

In order for Case Western Reserve University to issue an check to you
I must give them your social security number.

What is your social security number?   _____-_____-_____

You can expect the check within the next couple of weeks. Thank you
again. Bye.

APPENDIX B
FLYER ANNOUNCING THE STUDY TO CONGREGATE
MEAL ELDERS

WOULD YOU BE ABLE TO HELP ME?

WHO: My name is Valerie Brown and I am finishing my PH.D. in sociology at Case Western Reserve University.

WHAT: I need people 60 years of age and older who live in certain Cleveland neighborhoods to answer some questions about their neighborhoods and life in general.

WHEN: I or my assistant, Judie Barker, will call you and ask the questions over the phone. It will take about 15 minutes of your time.

Because your time is valuable and we appreciate your help, Case Western Reserve University will give you $10.00 for answering the questions.

The staff at your local senior citizens center thought you might be interested in helping me. If you are called, *PLEASE SAY YES.*

99

WOULD YOU BE ABLE TO HELP ME?

WHO: My name is Valerie Brown and I am finishing my PH.D. in sociology at Case Western Reserve University.

WHAT: I need people 60 years of age and older who live in certain Cleveland neighborhoods to answer some questions about their neighborhoods and life in general.

WHEN: I or my assistant, Judie Barker, will call you and ask the questions over the phone. It will take about 15 minutes of your time.

Because your time is valuable and we appreciate your help, Case Western Reserve University will give you $10.00 for answering the questions.

If you are interested in helping me, PLEASE CALL 368-2700 and leave your name, address and phone number for Valerie Brown.

Figure 1. Urban Ecological Model of Subjective Well-Being Among the Elderly

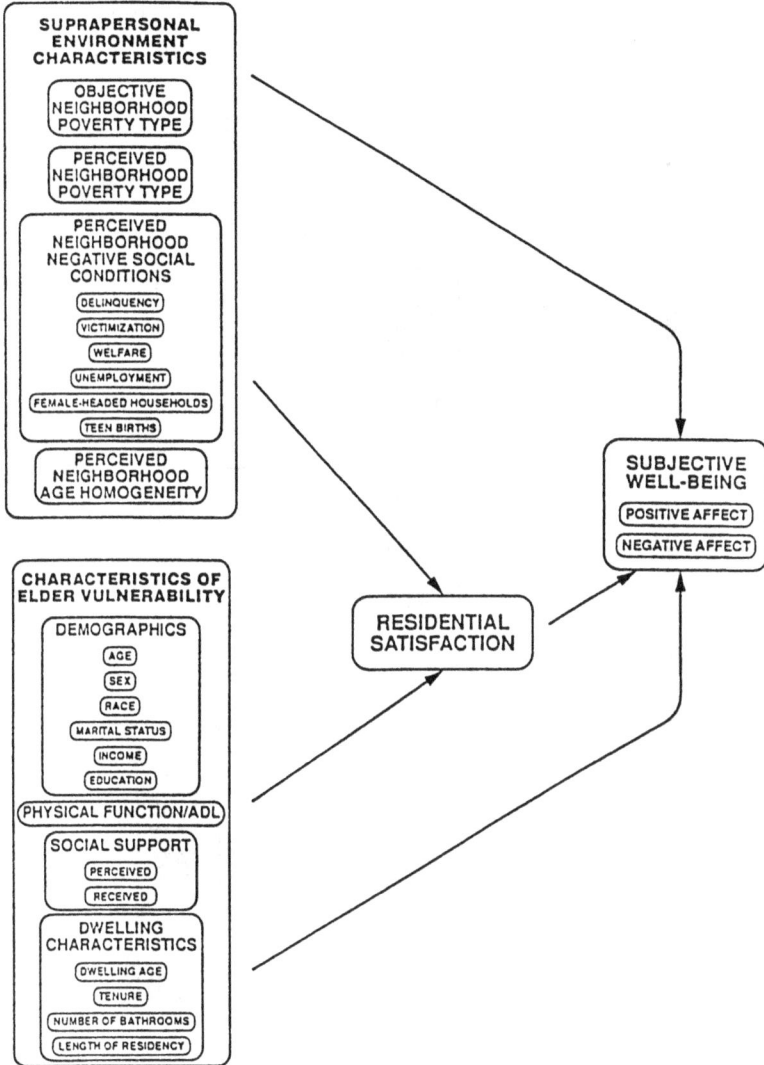

SUPRAPERSONAL ENVIRONMENT CHARACTERISTICS
- OBJECTIVE NEIGHBORHOOD POVERTY TYPE
- PERCEIVED NEIGHBORHOOD POVERTY TYPE
- PERCEIVED NEIGHBORHOOD NEGATIVE SOCIAL CONDITIONS
  - DELINQUENCY
  - VICTIMIZATION
  - WELFARE
  - UNEMPLOYMENT
  - FEMALE-HEADED HOUSEHOLDS
  - TEEN BIRTHS
- PERCEIVED NEIGHBORHOOD AGE HOMOGENEITY

CHARACTERISTICS OF ELDER VULNERABILITY
- DEMOGRAPHICS
  - AGE
  - SEX
  - RACE
  - MARITAL STATUS
  - INCOME
  - EDUCATION
- PHYSICAL FUNCTION/ADL
- SOCIAL SUPPORT
  - PERCEIVED
  - RECEIVED
- DWELLING CHARACTERISTICS
  - DWELLING AGE
  - TENURE
  - NUMBER OF BATHROOMS
  - LENGTH OF RESIDENCY

RESIDENTIAL SATISFACTION

SUBJECTIVE WELL-BEING
- POSITIVE AFFECT
- NEGATIVE AFFECT

Figure 2. Urban Ecological Interaction Model of Subjective
Well-Being Among the Elderly

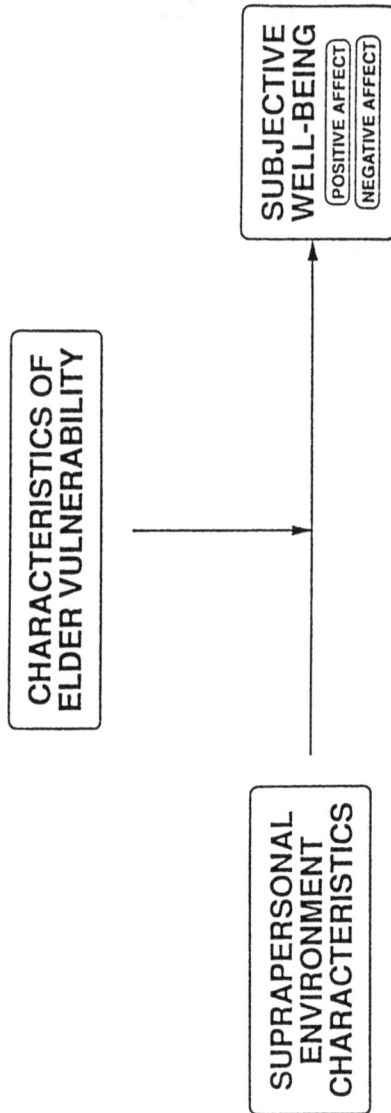

SUBJECTIVE
WELL-BEING

POSITIVE AFFECT
NEGATIVE AFFECT

CHARACTERISTICS OF
ELDER VULNERABILITY

SUPRAPERSONAL
ENVIRONMENT
CHARACTERISTICS

Figure 3. Hypothesized Effects of Suprapersonal Environment and Characteristics
of Elder Vulnerability on Subjective Well-Being

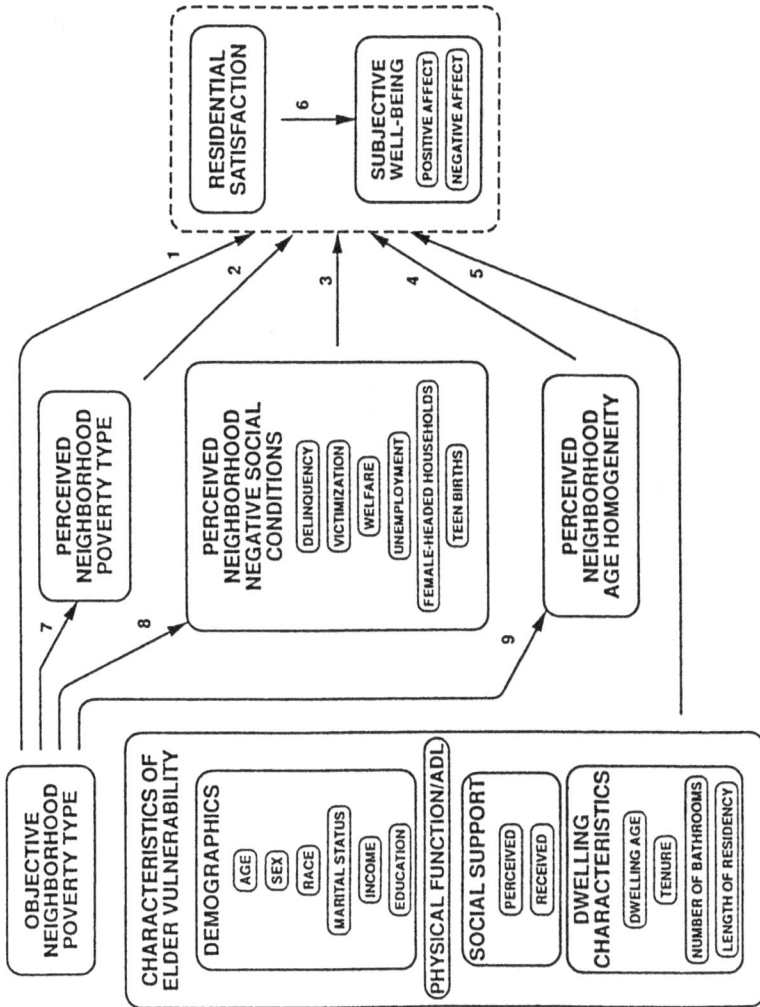

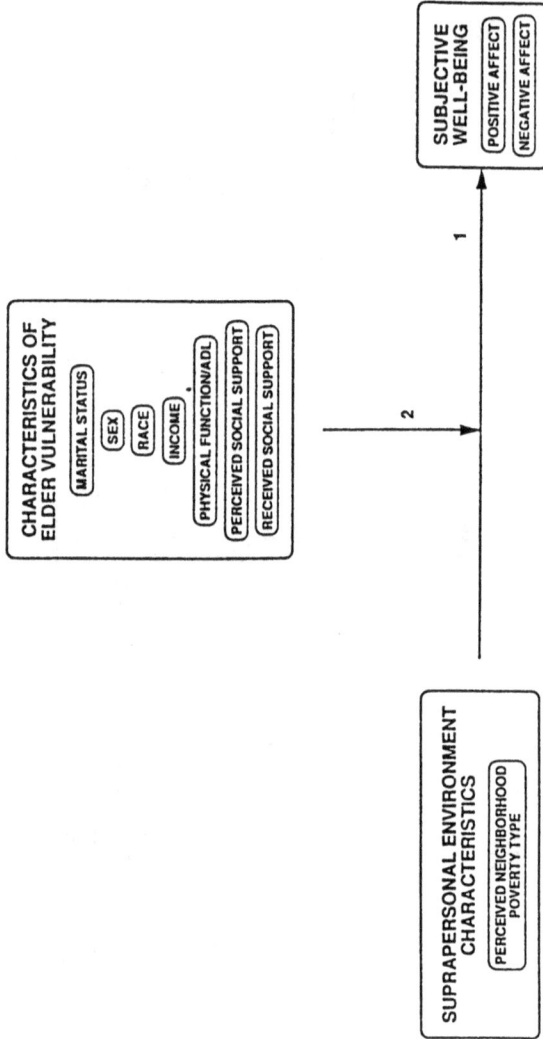

Figure 4. Hypothesized Interaction Effects of Suprapersonal Environment and Characteristics of Elder Vulnerability on Subjective Well-Being

Figure 5. Statistically Significant Effects of Suprapersonal Environment and Elder
Vulnerability Characteristics on Residential Satisfaction and Positive Affect[1,2]

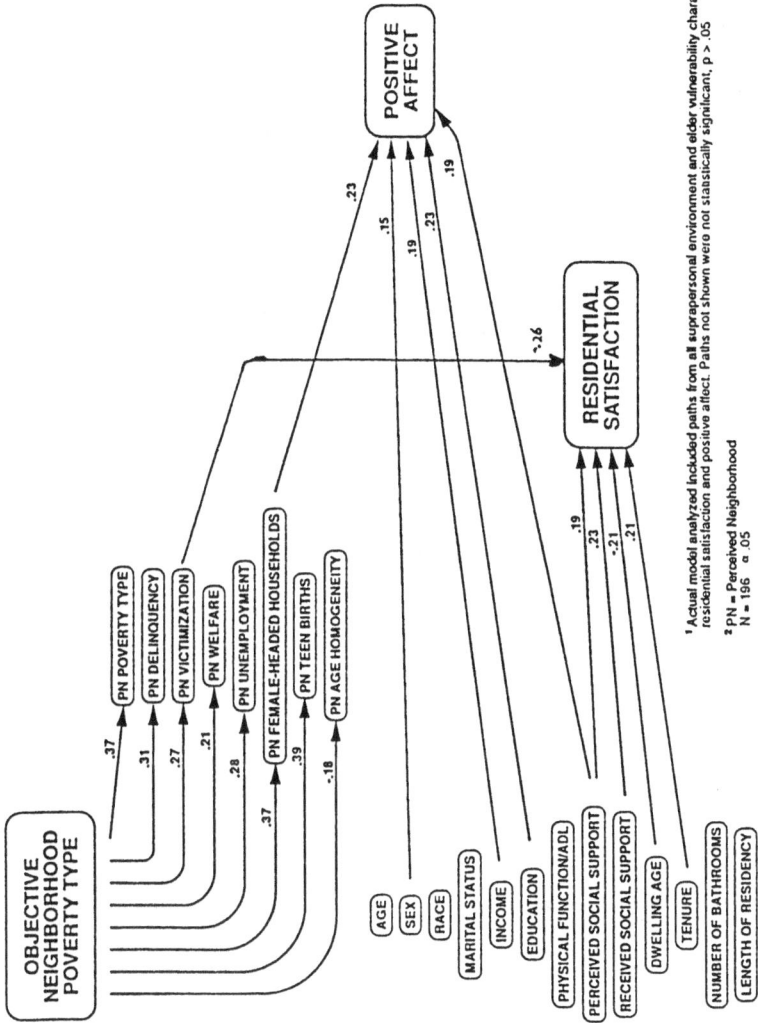

[1] Actual model analyzed included paths from all suprapersonal environment and elder vulnerability characteristics to residential satisfaction and positive affect. Paths not shown were not statsically significant, p > .05

[2] PN = Perceived Neighborhood
N = 196   α = .05

105

Figure 6. Statistically Significant Effects of Suprapersonal Environment and Elder Vulnerability Characteristics on Residential Satisfaction and Negative Affect[1,2]

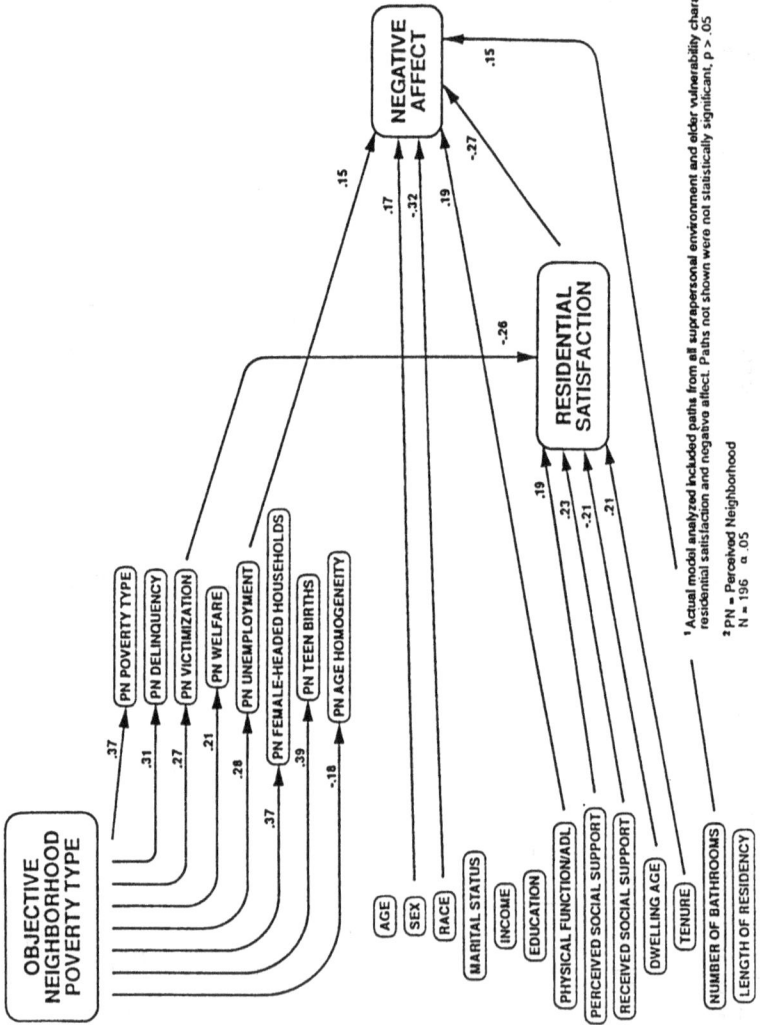

[1] Actual model analyzed included paths from all suprapersonal environment and elder vulnerability characteristics to residential satisfaction and negative affect. Paths not shown were not statistically significant, p > .05

[2] PN = Perceived Neighborhood
N = 196   α .05

106

Table 1

Actual Sampling Frame

Poverty Type	Census Tract	Neighborhood SPA[1]	Subjects
Traditional high poverty (all East Side) n = 55	1089	Central	12
	1126	Hough	12
	1128	Hough	9
	1143	Kinsman	12
	1189	Hough	10
New high poverty (all East Side) n = 37	1119	St. Clair/Superior	10
	1129	Central	5
	1132	Fairfax	5
	1136	Fairfax	11
	1148	Kinsman	6
Emerging high poverty (3 East Side, 6 West Side)	1117	St. Clair/Superior	12
	1142	Central	11
	1165	Glenville	8
	1047.02	Tremont	11
	1042	Tremont	1
	1043	Tremont	2
	1044	Tremont	3
	1045	Tremont	1
	1038	Ohio City/Near West Side	1
Low poverty (3 East Side, 2 West Side)	1172.01	S. Collinwood	12
	1175	N. Collinwood	12
	1149	N. Broadway	12
	1244	Puritas/Longmead	12
	1246	Puritus/Longmead	6

N = 196

[1] SPA is statistical planning area

		TABLE 2			
	Zero-order Correlation and Univariate Statistics[1,2]				
	1	2	3	4	5
1. Positive affect	—	.28	-.11	.06	.04
2. Negative affect	.28	—	-.42	.07	.09
3. Residential satisfaction	-.11	-.42	—	-.19	-.17
4. Objective neighborhood poverty type	.06	.07	-.19	—	.37
5. Perceived neighborhood poverty type	.04	.09	-.17	.37	—
6. Juvenile delinquency	.06	.28	-.33	.31	.27
7. Welfare assistance	.05	.12	-.23	.21	.33
8. Teen births	.12	.23	-.33	.39	.28
9. Victimization of neighbors	.18	.33	-.38	.27	.30
10. Female-headed households	.30	.18	-.28	.37	.28
11. Unemployment	.21	.23	-.14	.28	.09
12. Neighborhood age homogeneity	-.07	-.06	.16	-.18	-.04
13. Age	-.10	-.08	.15	-.10	-.11
14. Race	-.05	-.08	-.13	.66	.27
15. Sex	.07	.09	.01	.08	.09
16. Marital status	.06	-.01	-.01	.05	-.06
17. Education	.38	-.02	-.04	-.06	-.08
18. Income	.19	.04	.04	-.17	-.10
19. ADL	-.03	.28	-.18	.05	.15
20. Perceived social support	.20	-.27	.28	.18	-.11
21. Received social support	.11	-.07	.17	.01	-.06
22. Age of dwelling	-.14	-.07	-.11	-.10	.00
23. Home ownership	-.06	-.17	.14	-.19	-.06
24. Number of bathrooms	.07	.08	-.02	.02	-.03
25. Length of residency	-.07	-.06	.03	-.13	-.14
MEAN	14.0	14.6	.00		
SD	4.7	4.8	4.5		
SKEW	.21	.68	-1.2		
KURTOSIS	-.85	-.38	1.0		
MISSING	0	0	1	0	53

TABLE 2 (Continued)
Zero-order Correlation and Univariate Statistics

	6	7	8	9	10
1. Positive affect	.06	.05	.12	.18	.30
2. Negative affect	.28	0.12	.23	.33	.18
3. Residential satisfaction	-.33	-.23	-.33	-.38	-.28
4. Objective neighborhood poverty type	.31	.21	.39	.27	.37
5. Perceived neighborhood poverty type	.27	.33	.28	.30	.28
6. Juvenile delinquency	—	.46	.45	.62	.44
7. Welfare assistance	.46	—	.50	.35	.42
8. Teen births	.45	.50	—	.51	.50
9. Victimization of neighbors	.62	.35	.51	—	.51
10. Female-headed households	.44	.42	.50	.51	—
11. Unemployment	.24	.31	.40	.35	.34
12. Neighborhood age homogeneity	-.10	-.15	-.16	-.07	-.23
13. Age	-.11	-.12	-.16	-.08	-.08
14. Race	.18	.18	.36	.16	.25
15. Sex	.07	-.02	.01	.00	.03
16. Marital status	.00	-.02	.04	-.04	.16
17. Education	-.11	-.11	-.01	-.06	.08
18. Income	-.14	-.19	-.11	-.13	-.12
19. ADL	.04	.13	.08	.03	.05
20. Perceived social support	-.17	-.22	-.15	-.11	-.01
21. Received social support	.04	-.01	.04	.02	.16
22. Age of dwelling	.02	-.02	.00	-.09	-.11
23. Home ownership	-.06	-.08	-.13	-.08	-.03
24. Number of bathrooms	-.01	-.10	-.16	.04	-.06
25. Length of residency	-.06	-.19	-.10	-.06	-.10
MEAN	37.8	57.9	27.4	30.4	37.8
SD	34.6	33.0	31.1	30.5	35.2
SKEW	.38	-.27	1.0	.68	.49
KURTOSIS	-1.3	-1.2	-.18	-.81	-1.2
MISSING	38	40	53	34	57

109

	TABLE 2 (Continued) Zero-Correlation and Univariate Statistics[1,2]				
	11	12	13	14	15
1. Positive affect	.21	-.07	-.10	-.05	.07
2. Negative affect	.23	-.06	-.08	-.08	.09
3. Residential satisfaction	-.14	.16	.15	-.13	.01
4. Objective neighborhood poverty type	.28	-.18	-.10	.66	.08
5. Perceived neighborhood poverty type	.09	-.04	-.11	.27	.09
6. Juvenile delinquency	.24	-.10	-.11	.18	.07
7. Welfare assistance	.31	-.15	-.12	.18	-.02
8. Teen births	.40	-.16	-.16	.36	.01
9. Victimization of neighbors	.38	-.07	-.08	.16	.00
1. Female-headed households	.34	-.23	-.08	.25	.03
11. Unemployment	—	-.05	.02	.20	.03
12. Neighborhood age homogeneity	-.05	—	.11	-.04	.03
13. Age	.02	.11	—	-.12	.06
14. Race	.20	-.04	-.12	—	.10
15. Sex	.03	.03	.06	.10	—
16. Marital status	.05	-.04	.10	.00	.27
17. Education	.04	-.13	-.25	-.11	-.02
18. Income	-.05	.05	.16	-.27	-.24
19. ADL	.07	-.11	.09	.05	-.03
2. Perceived social support	.05	-.01	.13	.09	.00
21. Received social support	.10	-.16	-.09	.05	-.04
22. Age of dwelling	-.06	-.04	.03	-.17	-.04
23. Home ownership	-.15	-.03	.09	-.19	-.05
24. Number of bathrooms	-.07	-.08	.02	-.01	-.09
25. Length of residency	-.04	.07	.24	-.29	.02
X	37.9		73.0		
SD	33.9		8.1		
SKEW	.42		.64		
KURTOSIS	-1.2		-.17		
MISSING	50	6	0	1	0

	16	17	18	19	20
TABLE 2 (Continued) Zero-order Correlation and Univariate Statistics					
1. Positive affect	.06	.33	.19	-.03	.20
2. Negative affect	-.01	-.02	.04	.28	-.27
3. Residential satisfaction	-.01	-.04	.04	-.18	.28
4. Objective neighborhood poverty type	.05	-.06	-.17	.05	.18
5. Perceived neighborhood poverty type	-.06	-.08	-.10	.15	-.11
6. Juvenile delinquency	.00	-.11	-.14	.04	-.17
7. Welfare assistance	-.02	-.11	-.19	.13	-.22
8. Teen births	.04	-.01	-.11	.08	-.15
9. Victimization of neighbors	-.04	-.06	-.13	.03	-.11
10. Female-headed households	.16	.08	-.12	.05	-.01
11. Unemployment	.05	.04	-.05	.07	.05
12. Neighborhood age homogeneity	-.04	-.13	.05	-.11	-.01
13. Age	.10	-.25	.12	.09	.13
14. Race	.00	-.11	-.27	.05	.09
15. Sex	.27	-.02	-.24	-.03	.00
16. Marital status	—	-.01	-.10	-.06	.07
17. Education	-.01	—	.22	-.10	.20
18. Income	-.10	.22	—	-.02	.06
19. ADL	-.06	-.10	-.02	—	-.23
20. Perceived social support	.07	-.20	.06	-.23	—
21. Received social support	.04	.15	.05	.01	.19
22. Age of dwelling	-.13	-.07	.18	-.02	-.08
23. Home ownership	-.29	-.08	.12	-.09	-.09
24. Number of bathrooms	-.13	-.03	.08	.01	-.02
25. Length of residency	-.21	-.06	.22	-.13	-.03
MEAN		3.1	1.8	14.7	22.10
SD		1.2	1.0	6.8	3.30
SKEW				.64	-.27
KURTOSIS				-.59	.16
MISSING	0	1	16	4	0

	21	22	23	24	25
TABLE 2 (Continued) Zero-order Correlation and Univariate Statistics[1,2]					
1. Positive affect	.11	-.14	-.06	.07	-.07
2. Negative affect	-.07	-.07	-.17	.08	-.06
3. Residential satisfaction	.17	-.11	.14	-.02	.03
4. Objective neighborhood poverty type	.01	-.10	-.19	.02	-.13
5. Perceived neighborhood poverty type	-.06	.00	-.06	-.03	-.14
6. Juvenile delinquency	.04	.02	-.06	-.01	-.06
7. Welfare assistance	-.01	-.02	-.08	-.10	-.19
8. Teen births	.04	.00	-.13	-.16	-.10
9. Victimization of neighbors	.02	-.09	-.08	.04	-.06
10. Female-headed households	.16	-.11	-.03	-.06	-.10
11. Unemployment	.10	-.06	-.15	-.07	-.04
12. Neighborhood age homogeneity	-.16	-.04	-.03	-.08	.07
13. Age	-.09	.03	.09	.02	.24
14. Race	.05	-.17	-.19	-.01	-.29
15. Sex	-.04	-.04	-.05	-.09	.02
16. Marital status	.04	-.13	-.29	-.13	-.21
17. Education	.15	-.07	-.08	-.03	-.06
18. Income	.05	.18	.12	.08	.22
19. ADL	.01	-.02	-.09	.01	-.13
20. Perceived social support	.19	-.08	-.09	-.02	-.03
21. Received social support	—	.08	-.03	-.03	.00
22. Age of dwelling	.08	—	.37	.18	.39
23. Home ownership	-.03	.37	—	.30	.47
24. Number of bathrooms	-.03	.18	.30	—	.19
25. Length of residency	.00	.39	.47	.19	—
MEAN	17.1	5.6		1.1	21.8
SD	4.7	.8		.4	17.1
SKEW	.23			2.3	.84
KURTOSIS	-.54			4.7	.14
MISSING	1	3	0	1	2

[1]Mean substitution used for missing values to calculate zero-order correlation.

[2]Shaded areas are correlations that are statistically significant; p < .05

		Table 3 Regression Results for Direct and Interaction Effects on PA, NA, and Residential Satisfaction[1,2]				
	Positive Affect		Negative Affect		Residential Satisfaction	
	b	Beta	b	Beta	b	Beta
Suprapersonal Environment						
Objective poverty type	-.06	-.02	.38	.09	-.08	-.02
Perceived poverty type	.08	.02	-.18	-.04	.23	.05
Juvenile delinquency	-.01	-.06	.01	.08	-.01	-.07
Welfare assistance	0	.01	-.02	-.13	0	.01
Births to teens	.01	.04	.02	.12	-.01	-.03
Victimization	.01	.06	.01	.08	-.05	-.26
Female Headed Households	.04	.23	.01	.04	-.02	-.12
Unemployment	.02	.11	.02	.15	.01	.04
Neighborhood Age Homogeneity	.44	.05	.30	.03	1.07	.11
Characteristics of Elder Vulnerability						
Age	-.04	-.06	-.04	-.07	.05	.08
Sex (female = higher)	1.81	.15	2.20	.17	.39	.03
Race (black = higher)	-1.53	-.16	-3.20	-.32	-.94	-.09
Marital status (non-married = higher)	-.13	-.01	-1.10	-.09	-.30	-.02
Education	.94	.23	-.32	-.08	.47	-.11
Income	.90	.19	.52	.11	-.08	-.02
ADL	-.01	-.01	.13	.19	-.10	-.13
Perceived Support	.27	.19	-.19	-.13	.28	.19
Received Support	.03	.04	0	0	.24	.23
Dwelling age	-.84	-.15	-.64	-.11	-1.26	-.21
Tenure (owner = higher)	.26	.03	-1.3	-.13	2.09	.21
Number of bathrooms	1.75	.14	1.97	.15	-.13	-.01
Length of residency	-.02	-.07	-.02	-.07	-.02	-.08
Residential Satisfaction	-.10	-.10	-.27	-.27	—	—

[1]Mean substitution used for missing values in the regression analysis

[2]Shaded areas are Betas that are statistically significant: p < .05

113

Table 3 (Continued) Regression Results for Direct and Interaction Effects on PA, NA, and Residential Staisfaction[1,2]			
Interaction for Perceived Neighborhood Poverty Type by Elder Vulnerability	Positive Affect	Negative Affect	Residential Satisfaction
PT2 X SEX	-.15	-.56	—
PT2 X RACE	.75	.33	—
PT2 X MSTAT	-.41	1.04	—
PT2 X ADL	-.04	.05	—
PT2 X INCOME	.39	.04	—
PT2 X PVSUP	-.06	.10	—
PT2 X RVSUP	-.08	-.03	—
Main Effects			
Adjusted R^2	.25	.32	.28
F	3.80	5.07	4.42
df	23,172	23,172	22,173
P	<.0001	<.0001	<.0001
Interaction Effects			
R^2 Change	.02, p > .05	.02, p > .05	—
Adjusted R^2	.24	.32	—
F	3.09	4.06	—
df	30,165	30,165	—
P	<.0001	<.0001	
			N = 196

PT2 x RACE = perceived poverty type x race
PT2 X ADL = perceived poverty type x ADL
PT2 X PVSUP = perceived poverty type x Perceived support
PT2 X RVSUP = perceived poverty type x Received support
PT2 X SEX = perceived poverty type x sex
PT2 X MSTAT = perceived poverty type x marital status

114

TABLE 4

Decomposition of Effects of Suprapersonal Environment
and Elder Vulnerability Characteristics on Residential Satisfaction and PA and NA
(Standardized Values)[a]

Dependent Variable, Independent Variable	Direct	Indirect	Total
PN Poverty type, Objective Neighborhood Poverty Type	.37	0	.37
PN Delinquency, Objective Neighborhood Poverty Type	.31	0	.31
PN Victimization, Objective Neighborhood Poverty Type	.27	0	.27
PN Welfare, Objective Neighborhood Poverty Type	.21	0	.21
PN Unemployment, Objective Neighborhood Poverty Type	.28	0	.28
PN Female-headed Households, Objective Neighborhood Poverty Type	.37	0	.37
PN Teen births, Objective Neighborhood Poverty Type	.39	0	.39
PN Age Homogeneity, Objective Neighborhood Poverty Type	-.18	0	-.18
Residential Satisfaction, PN Poverty Type	0	0	0
Residential Satisfaction, PN Delinquency	0	0	0
Residential Satisfaction, PN Victimization	-.26	0	-.26
Residential Satisfaction, PN Welfare	0	0	0
Residential Satisfaction, PN Unemployment	0	0	0
Residential Satisfaction, PN Female-Headed Households	0	0	0
Residential Satisfaction, PN Teen Births	0	0	0
Residential Satisfaction, PN Age Homogeneity	0	0	0
Residential Satisfaction, Objective Neighborhood Poverty Type	0	-.07	-.07
Residential Satisfaction, Age	0	0	0
Residential Satisfaction, Sex	0	0	0
Residential Satisfaction, Race	0	0	0
Residential Satisfaction, Marital Status	0	0	0
Residential Satisfaction, Income	0	0	0
Residential Satisfaction, Education	0	0	0
Residential Satisfaction, Physical Function/ADL	0	0	0
Residential Satisfaction, Perceived Social Support	.19	0	.19
Residential Satisfaction, Received Social Support	.23	0	.23
Residential Satisfaction, Dwelling Age	-.21	0	-.21

Dependent Variable, Independent Variable	Direct	Indirect	Total
TABLE 4 (Continued) Decomposition of Effects of Suprapersonal Environment and Elder Vulnerability characteristics on Residential Satisfaction and PA and NA (Standardized Values)[a]			
Residential Satisfaction, Tenure (Home Ownership)	.21	0	.21
Residential Satisfaction, Number of Bathrooms	0	0	0
Residential Satisfaction, Length of Residency	0	0	0
Positive Affect, Residential Satisfaction	0	0	0
Positive Affect, PN Poverty Type	0	0	0
Positive Affect, PN Delinquency	0	0	0
Positive Affect, PN Victimization	0	0	0
Positive Affect, PN Welfare	0	0	0
Positive Affect, PN Unemployment	0	0	0
Positive Affect, PN Female-headed Households	.23	0	.23
Positive Affect, PN Teen Births	0	0	0
Positive Affect, PN Age Homogeneity	0	0	0
Positive Affect, Objective Neighborhood Poverty Type	0	.09	.09
Positive Affect, Age	0	0	0
Positive Affect, Sex	.15	0	.15
Positive Affect, Race	0	0	0
Positive Affect, Marital Status	0	0	0
Positive Affect, Income	.19	0	.19
Positive Affect, Education	.23	0	.23
Positive Affect, Physical Function/ADL	0	0	0
Positive Affect, Perceived Social Support	.19	0	.19
Positive Affect, Received Social Support	0	0	0
Positive Affect, Dwelling Age	0	0	0
Positive Affect, Tenure (Home Ownership)	0	0	0
Positive Affect, Number of Bathrooms	0	0	0
Positive Affect, Length of Residency	0	0	0
Negative Affect, Residential Satisfaction	-.27	0	-.27

TABLE 4 (Continued)
Decomposition of Effects of Suprapersonal Environment
and Elder Vulnerability characteristics on Residential Satisfaction and PA and NA
(Standardized Values)[*]

Dependent Variable, Independent Variable	Direct	Indirect	Total
Negative Affect, PN Poverty Type	0	0	0
Negative Affect, PN Delinquency	0	0	0
Negative Affect, PN Victimization	0	.07	.07
Negative Affect, PN Welfare	0	0	0
Negative Affect, PN Unemployment	.15	0	.15
Negative Affect, PN Female-headed Households	0	0	0
Negative Affect, PN Teen Bu ...	0	0	0
Negative Affect, PN Age Hou:.	0	0	0
Negative Affect, Objective Neighborhood Poverty Type	0	.06	.06
Negative Affect, Age	0	0	0
Negative Affect, Sex	.17	0	.17
Negative Affect, Race	-.32	0	-.32
Negative Affect, Marital Status	0	0	0
Negative Affect, Income	0	0	0
Negative Affect, Education	0	0	0
Negative Affect, Physical Function/ADL	.19	0	.19
Negative Affect, Perceived Social Support	0	-.05	-.05
Negative Affect, Received Social Support	0	-.06	-.06
Negative Affect, Dwelling Age	0	.06	.06
Negative Affect, Tenure (Home Ownership)	0	-.06	-.06
Negative Affect, Number of Bathrooms	.15	0	.15
Negative Affect, Length of Residency	0	0	0

[*] PN = Perceived Neighborhood

TABLE 5
Variable Frequencies According to Objective Neighborhood Poverty Type ᵃ

	High Poverty Type												Low Poverty Type (n = 56)			
	Traditional (n = 55)				New (n = 32)				Emerging (n = 50)							
	%	X	SD	n	%	X	SD	n	%	X	SD	n	%	X	SD	n
Suprapersonal Environment Characteristics																
PN Poverty Type																
Traditional	47			18	31			9	30			11	8			3
New	21			8	10			3	11			4	5			2
Emerging	26			10	44			13	35			13	39			15
Low	5			2	14			4	24			9	48			19
% PN Juvenile delinquency		55	35	38		44	33	34		72	33	43		22	29	43
% PN Welfare Assistance		67	32	41		62	29	33		59	33	43		44	34	39
% PN Teen Births		45	33	40		38	35	29		18	26	37		10	15	37
% PN Victimization		43	34	43		33	30	31		29	30	41		19	23	46
% PN Female-headed households		43	34	37		40	33	29		25	28	35		23	31	38
% PN Unemployment		37	35	38		37	34	31		31	30	40		27	29	37
PN Age Homogeneity																
mostly non-elderly	73			37	58			21	53			26	48			26
mostly elderly	27			14	42			15	47			23	52			23
Characteristics of Elder Vulnerability																
Age (years)		73	8	55		71	8	37		74	8	50		74	8	54
Sex																
Female	89			49	78			29	84			42	80			43
Male	11			6	22			8	16			8	20			11
Race																
Black	95			52	95			35	50			25	17			9
White	4			2	5			2	50			25	83			45
Marital Status																
Married	9			5	24			9	34			17	11			6
Non-Married	91			50	76			28	66			33	89			48

TABLE 5 (Continued)
Variable Frequencies According to Objective Neighborhood Poverty Type [a]

	High Poverty Type												Low Poverty Type (n = 54)			
	Traditional (n = 55)				New (n = 72)				Emerging (n = 50)							
	%	X	SD	n	%	X	SD	n	%	X	SD	n	%	X	SD	n
Education																
0-4 (Grade)	9			5	11			4	4			2	6			3
5-8	22			12	13			5	36			18	15			8
9-11	31			17	40			15	28			14	38			20
H.S.	25			14	30			11	28			14	26			14
Some College	9			5	3			1	4			2	7			4
BA	4			2	3			1	0			0	6			3
MA or more	0			0	0			0	0			0	2			1
Income																
$0-2,500	13			6	6			2	11			5	2			1
2,501-5,000	26			12	38			13	40			19	21			11
5,001-10,000	50			23	36			13	34			16	57			30
10,001-15,000	9			4	12			4	9			4	4			2
15,001-25,000	2			1	3			1	6			3	15			8
25,000 +	0			0	3			1	0			0	2			1
ADL		15	7	52		16	7	37		14	7	50		15	6	53
Perceived Social Support		23	4	55		21	3	37		21	3	50		22	3	54
Received Social Support		17	5	55		17	4	36		17	4	50		17	5	54
Dwelling Age (years)																
<1	0			0	0			0	0			0	0			0
1-5	0			0	0			0	0			0	0			0
6-10	6			3	0			0	4			2	2			1
11-20	23			12	5			2	6			3	17			9
21-30	6			3	5			2	6			3	2			1
31+	66			35	89			33	84			42	79			42
Tenure (Home Ownership)																
Non-Owner	75			41	60			22	36			18	56			30
Owner	25			14	40			15	64			32	44			24

| | High Poverty Type | | | | | | | | | | | | Low Poverty Type (n = 54) | | | |
| | Traditional (n = 55) | | | | New (n = 72) | | | | Emerging (n = 30) | | | | | | | |
	%	X	SD	n	%	X	SD	n	%	X	SD	n	%	X	SD	n
Number of Bathrooms																
1.0	89			48	73			27	82			41	83			45
1.5	4			2	0			0	8			4	7			4
2.0	4			2	27			10	10			5	9			5
2.5	2			1	0			0	0			0	0			0
3.0	2			1	0			0	0			0	0			0
Length of Residency		19	15	54		19	14	37		24	19	30		24	18	53
Residential Satisfaction		-.22	5	55		-3	6	37		.91	4	30		:	4	53
Positive Affect		15	5	55		14	4	37		13	5	30		14	5	54
Negative Affect		15	4	55		15	5	37		14	5	30		14	5	54

N = 136

[a] PN = Perceived Neighborhood

[b] Valid percent is presented in this table; i.e. missing cases are omitted from percent calculations; due to rounding, the sum of percentages may be greater than 100.

Table 6 Coding Scheme and Psychometric Properties of the Baseline Data[1]		
Variables	Coding Scheme	Psychometric Properties
Suprapersonal Environment Characteristics		
Objective neighborhood poverty type	4-point code based on Coulton typology (see text)	N/A
	0 = low poverty	
	1 = emerging high poverty	
	2 = new high poverty	
	3 = traditional high poverty	
PN poverty type	4-point code that corresponds to Coulton typology (see text) and based on respondent's estimation of degree and duration of neighborhood poverty.	N/A
	0 = low poverty	
	1 = emerging high poverty	
	2 = new high poverty	
	3 = traditional high poverty	
PN delinquency	Respondent's estimate of percent of persons in the neighborhood who display a given characteristic (eg. percent teenagers who are delinquent).	N/A
PN victimization		
PN welfare		
PN female-headed households		
PN unemployment		
PN teen births		
PN age homogeneity	Respondent's assessment of elders as majority age group in neighborhood.	N/A
	1 = mostly elderly	
	0 = not mostly elderly	

Variables	Coding Scheme	Psychometric Properties
TABLE 6 (Continued)		
Coding Scheme and Psychometric Properties of the Baseline Data[1]		
Characteristics of Elder Vulnerability		
Age	Actual age in years	N/A
Sex (female)	1 = yes, 0 = no	N/A
Race (black)	1 = yes, 0 = no	N/A
Marital Status (single)	1 = yes, 0 = no	N/A
Income	0 = ≤ $2,500	N/A
	1 = $2,501 - 5,000	
	2 = $5,001 - 10,000	
	3 = $10,001 - 15,000	
	4 = $15,001 - 25,000	
	5 = $25,001 +	
Education	1 = ≤ 4th grade	N/A
	2 = 5th - 8th grade	
	3 = 9th - 11th grade	
	4 = high school	
	5 = some college	
	6 = Bachelor's degree	
	7 = Master's degree or higher	
Physical function/ADL	Six - item scale: level of difficulty	alpha = .87
	1 = none	
	2 = a little	
	3 = some	
	4 = quite a bit	
	5 = very much	

TABLE 6 (Continued)
Coding Scheme and Psychometric Properties of the Baseline Data[1]

Variables	Coding Scheme	Psychometric Properties
Perceived Social Support*	Six-item scale	alpha = .68
	1 = strongly disagree	
	2 = disagree	
	3 = neither agree nor disagree	
	4 = agree	
	5 = strongly agree	
Received Social Support	Six-item scale	alpha = .69
	1 = never	
	2 = once in a while	
	3 = fairly often	
	4 = very often	
Dwelling Age	Actual age-range of home	N/A
	1 = less than one year	
	2 = 1-5 years	
	3 = 6-10 years	
	4 = 11-20 years	
	5 = 21-30 years	
	6 = 31+ years	
Tenure (home ownership)	1 = yes, 0 = no	N/A
Number of bathrooms	Actual number of bathrooms	N/A
Length of residency	Actual length of time reside in present home	N/A
Residential satisfaction*	Z-score composite of three subscales	alpha = .77
	Neighborhood satisfaction - 3 items	
	Housing satisfaction -2 items	
	Desire to move - 2 items	
	Coding for extent items	
	1 = not at all	
	2 = a little	
	3 = somewhat	

Variables	Coding Scheme	Psychometric Properties
	4 = quite a bit	
	5 = very much	
	Coding for level of agreement items	
	1 = strongly disagree	
	2 = disagree	
	3 = neither agree nor disagree	
	4 = agree	
	5 = strongly agree	
Positive Affect*	Five-item scale	alpha = .72
	Coding for extent items	
	1 = not at all	
	2 = a little	
	3 = somewhat	
	4 = quite a bit	
	5 = very much	
	Coding for level of agreement items	
	1 = strongly disagree	
	2 = disagree	
	3 = neither agree nor disagree	
	4 = agree	
	5 = strongly agree	
Negative Affect*	Six-item scale	
	Coding for extent items	alpha = .75
	1 = not at all	
	2 = a little	
	3 = somewhat	
	4 = quite a bit	
	5 = very much	
	Coding for level of agreement items	

TABLE 6 (Continued)
Coding Scheme and Psychometric Properties of the Baseline Data[1]

	TABLE 6 (Continued) Coding Scheme and Psychometric Properties of the Baseline Data[1]	
Variables	Coding Scheme	Psychometric Properties
	1 = strongly disagree	
	2 = disagree	
	3 = neither agree nor disagree	
	4 = agree	
	5 = strongly agree	

[1] PN = Perceived Neighborhood
* some items were reverse coded such that values were consistent with the value of the scale.

Index

For Product Safety Concerns and Information please contact our EU
representative GPSR@taylorandfrancis.com
Taylor & Francis Verlag GmbH, Kaufingerstraße 24, 80331 München, Germany